A Nurse in the Belfast Blitz

The Diary of Emma Duffin, 1939–42

Trevor Parkhill

NORTHERN IRELAND
WAR MEMORIAL

NORTHERN IRELAND WAR MEMORIAL

Published in 2016 by
Northern Ireland War Memorial
21 Talbot Street Belfast BT1 2LD

www.niwarmemorial.org

ISBN 978-0-9929301-6-5

Design by John McMillan

Printed by GPS Colour Graphics Ltd

Picture Credits

Every attempt has been made to contact picture credit holders. Credits are noted by the relevant picture. If there is no picture credit the picture belongs to the NIWM collection or is in the public domain.

For their assistance with images, NIWM would like to thank the following: The Deputy Keeper of the Records at the Public Record Office of Northern Ireland, the Belfast Telegraph, the Royal Society for the Prevention of Accidents, Isabel Apsley, Inver Museum Collection of St John Ambulance Memorabilia, Special Collections at Queen's University Belfast, the Department of the Environment: Historic Environment Division, Stranmillis University College Belfast, the Imperial War Museums, and the Glenravel Local History Project (North Belfast).

Notes on diary and editorial practice

Emma Duffin's diary, amounting to some 138 closely-written manuscript pages in one volume (PRONI D2109/18/9) has been transcribed and is represented here almost exactly as it was written. Words that have been accidentally omitted in the original have, with a view to improving the sense, been inserted in square brackets. Abbreviations such as VAD, ATS etc are represented in the general introduction and chapter introductions without stops. In the diary transcription, however, the original format – V.A.D., A.T.S. etc – has been retained.

The first 130 pages appear to have been written as one continuous series of entries, though not on a daily basis, from the summer of 1939, with no apparent breaks until, as far as can be established, late 1942 or early 1943. In 1967 Miss Duffin added a further eight pages, accounting for the period between the end of diary entries and her demobilisation in 1944.

To facilitate accessibility, the text has been divided into five chapters, each with a short contextual introduction.

Original spellings have been retained. Czechoslovakia for example is sometimes represented as 'Czecho Slovakia' or 'Czecho-Slovakia'; spellings such as 'torpedoe', 'aeroplane' and 'realize /realized' are as in the original.

Where possible information is given in footnotes about family members, friends and acquaintances who are referred to only by their first name.

The many abbreviations and capitals, principally for military terms, are explained in the 'Abbreviations' page.

Contents

Acknowledgements

I owe a significant debt of gratitude to the Duffin family for their permission to reproduce Emma's diary and for their constant help with family details. In this context the contribution of Michael Duffin, Anne Blood and Dawn Gordon has been exemplary (as indeed was the case for the publication, in 2014, of Emma's First World War diaries).

I am much indebted to John McMillan for his design expertise, evident throughout the book, and to Bryan Rutledge who photographed items in the NIWM collection.

I should like to acknowledge the dedicated help and thoughtful assistance provided by Jenny Haslett and her colleagues in the Northern Ireland War Memorial, particularly Ciaran Elizabeth Doran, Victoria Gibson, Kerry McIvor, Bill Porter and the Chairman, Ian Wilson, who favoured the idea of publication when first I broached it. Lisa Lavery's research on suitable imagery was invaluable.

I remain grateful to PRONI staff, particularly Gemma Eaton and Ian Montgomery and my former colleague, now retired, Patricia Kernaghan, for their informed interest in making more generally accessible this important Second World War source. I would also like to renew my thanks to the Repository staff for their reliable service.

Chris Anderson and John McMullan at Bryson Charitable Group, Bryson House, Belfast, Jemma Lee, Archivist, British Red Cross, and Rachel Roberts, Archivist, Cheltenham Ladies' College, responded promptly and purposefully to my research requests.

I am glad to acknowledge with gratitude the observations, advice and help offered by Isabel Apsley, Jonathan Bardon, Tom Bartlett, Brian Barton, Baroness May Blood, Alun Evans, Brendan Fulton, Maud Hamill, Carmel Gallagher, Patricia Kelly, Norman McFadden, Kathryn McKelvey, Richard McMinn, Eamon Phoenix, Vivienne Pollock, Peter Roebuck, Bert Smyth, Revd David Steers, Eileen Thomson and Lucy Wray.

My wife Sheila has, in addition to her inestimable moral support and encouragement, doubled as a proof-reading and indexing critical friend.

Any shortcomings in this book are my responsibility entirely.

Trevor Parkhill

Foreword

Among the aims of the Northern Ireland War Memorial is to commemorate those men and women who contributed on the Home Front in both world wars. In all the selfless and valuable roles, that of nurses has probably never been given the attention and great credit it deserves. We are therefore delighted to be able to present another in our series of publications, which reflects the subject from a first-hand perspective: the personal diaries of the distinguished nurse Emma Duffin.

While the central drama of her Second World War experiences comes in the German air raids on Belfast in April and May 1941, there is immense interest throughout in her depiction, often forthright, of everyday life in the nursing sphere. Like untold numbers of citizens 'doing their bit', wartime life was often monotonous and wearying. Emma describes her time training in Aldershot; dismal weather, poor food and bleak accommodation. As Emma describes her time spent in Stranmillis Military Hospital, a theme throughout is the struggle with hospital administration and bureaucracy.

This was the reality for millions; dull, unglamorous work in a world of rationing and privation, interspersed for some with moments of high drama, perhaps mortal danger. For Emma Duffin, that was the Belfast Blitz, recorded so vividly and movingly here.

Trevor Parkhill must be congratulated for his diligent editing of, and commenting on, these absorbing wartime diaries. Perhaps the most telling insight Emma Duffin gives repeatedly is that despite the worries and losses, she never heard anyone doubt that Nazism would be defeated! It is this struggle that the Northern Ireland War Memorial has a duty to commemorate.

Ian Wilson
Chairman, Northern Ireland War Memorial

Emma Duffin
1916

Abbreviations

ACI	Army Council Instructions
ADMS	Assistant Director of Medical Services
AF	Army Forms
ARP	Air Raid Precautions
ATS	Auxiliary Territorial Service, the women's wing of the armed services.
BBC	British Broadcasting Corporation
BCSW	Belfast Council of Social Welfare
CCS	Central Clearing Station, first-aid/triage post close to the front line
CO	Commanding Officer
Col.	Colonel
Coy	Company
DMO	District Medical Officer
DMS	Director of Medical Services
FANY	First Aid Nursing Yeomanry, *Fannies*, formed in 1907
GOC	General Officer Commanding
MO	Medical Officer
NAAFI	Navy Army and Air Force Institutes
NCO	Non-commissioned officer
OC	Officer Commanding
QM	Quartermaster
RAF	Royal Air Force
RAMC	Royal Army Medical Corps
RASC	Royal Army Service Corps
Red X	Red Cross
Sgt	Sergeant
TAB	Typhoid A and B (vaccine)
VAD	Voluntary Aid Detachment nurse, a generally unqualified volunteer.
WAAC	The Women's Auxiliary Army Corps, formed in 1916
w.e.f.	with effect from
WO	War Office
WAAF	Women's Auxiliary Air Force
WRAC	Women's Royal Army Corps
WVS	Women's Voluntary Services

TO
MY MOTHER RACHEL
AND SISTER VALERIE
FOR THEIR DEDICATED CARE
OF MY BROTHER MAURICE

AND IN MEMORY OF MY FATHER
ALBERT PARKHILL
(1920–1994)

NURSING SERVICES

Introduction

A Nurse in the Belfast Blitz *The diary of Emma Duffin 1939–42*

Early in 1940 Emma Duffin (1883–1979)[1] accepted her appointment as Commandant of the Voluntary Aid Detachment (VAD) unit of Stranmillis Military Hospital, established in south Belfast on the outbreak of war in September 1939. This might well be seen as a natural continuation of the commitment she had shown to the caring side of the armed services a quarter of a century earlier, during the First World War. She had served abroad as VAD nurse for four years 1915–19, first in Alexandria, Egypt and then, from 1916, in northern France. For her dedicated service, always in conditions of hardship, Emma was mentioned in dispatches on 31 December 1918 before being demobbed in early 1919 (she had stayed on in northern France to attend to hospital staff and soldiers alike afflicted by the Spanish flu epidemic that characterised the last few months of hostilities and beyond).[2]

On returning to Belfast Emma rejoined her family in *Dunowen*, a house on Cliftonville Road in north Belfast. Her father, Adam, a prosperous businessman who had also been politically active as a Unionist representative for nigh on thirty years before the war, continued his political involvement in the post-Partition government of the newly-created Northern Ireland, serving as a Senator until his death, aged 83, in 1924. The Duffin family subsequently moved to *Summerhill*, a smaller though still spacious town house at Mount Pleasant off Stranmillis Road in the south of the city.

Emma Duffin (in centre) at No. 15 General Hospital, Alexandria, Egypt, 1915-16, flanked by a fellow VAD nurse, S. Williams, and an orderly, Mooney.

facing
Stained glass war memorial window
by Stanley Murray Scott

---

[1] Emma Sylvia Duffin b. Belfast 8 November 1883, d. Downpatrick 31 January 1979, buried Newcastle Co. Down.

[2] There are 5 of Emma Duffin's First World War diaries in the Public Record Office of Northern Ireland (PRONI), D2109/18/4, 5A, 5B, 6, and 7. They have been published as Trevor Parkhill, ed., *The First World War Diaries of Emma Duffin, Belfast Voluntary Aid Detachment Nurse, 1915–19* (Dublin, 2014).

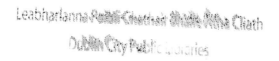

2

Three of Emma's six sisters – Dorothy, Celia and Molly – had also served in a VAD capacity, all of them at military hospital bases in England (though Molly completed her service in Bangor, Co. Down) and one of her two brothers, Terence, was awarded the Military Cross (and bar) while serving in the 36th Ulster Division. One of Emma's preoccupations on her return home had been the writing up of her wartime experiences while they were still fresh in her mind (though, as she describes them, most were utterly unforgettable). When war with Germany was declared on 3 September 1939 she wrote:

> *During the 1914–18 war I kept a diary … written while all the events were fresh in my mind and may some day be of interest. It is unlikely that in this war I will be able to take any active part…. On this account this diary will probably be less interesting and I may later decide that it is not worth keeping, but I will begin by recording some of our impressions before and on the outbreak of war.[3]*

PRONI D2109/20/1

Major Terence Duffin M.C. (and Bar). Emma's brother decorated for heroism in the First World War.

Letters of condolence to Mrs Maria Duffin on the death in 1936 of her son Terence.

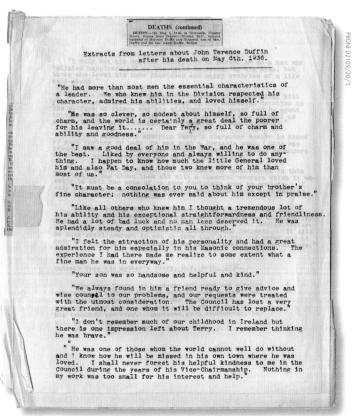

PRONI D2109/20/1

DEATHS (continued)

DUFFIN.—On May 6, 1936, at Newcastle, County Down, Major John Terence Duffin, M.C., beloved husband of Dorothy Duffin (née Sinclair), son of Mrs. Duffin and the late Adam Duffin, Belfast.

Extracts from letters about John Terence Duffin after his death on May 6th, 1936.

"He had more than most men the essential characteristics of a leader. We who knew him in the Division respected his character, admired his abilities, and loved himself."

"He was so clever, so modest about himself, so full of charm, and the world is certainly a great deal the poorer for his leaving it…….. Dear Tery, so full of charm and ability and goodness."

"I saw a good deal of him in the War, and he was one of the best. Liked by everyone and always willing to do anything. I happen to know how much the little General loved him and also Pat Day, and those two knew more of him than most of us."

"It must be a consolation to you to think of your brother's fine character; nothing was ever said about him except in praise."

"Like all others who knew him I thought a tremendous lot of his ability and his exceptional straightforwardness and friendliness. He had a lot of bad luck and no man less deserved it. He was splendidly steady and optimistic all through."

"I felt the attraction of his personality and had a great admiration for him especially in his Masonic connections. The experience I had there made me realize to some extent what a fine man he was in everyway."

"Your son was so handsome and helpful and kind."

"We always found in him a friend ready to give advice and wise counsel to our problems, and our requests were treated with the utmost consideration. The Council has lost a very great friend, and one whom it will be difficult to replace."

"I don't remember much of our childhood in Ireland but there is one impression left about Terry. I remember thinking he was brave."

"He was one of those whom the world cannot well do without and I know how he will be missed in his own town where he was loved. I shall never forget his helpful kindness to me in the Council during the years of his Vice-Chairmanship. Nothing in my work was too small for his interest and help."

[3] PRONI, D2109/18/9 p.1

Belfast Council of Social Welfare

Emma's mother, Maria, had been a founding member in 1906 of the Charity Organisation Society which became, in 1919, the Belfast Council of Social Welfare, a body which 'saw its role in training and advising poor people on ways to restore their independence…. [working] largely with dependent groups … such as children, widows and older people'.[4] In the early 1920s, Emma joined her mother on the executive committee, attending monthly policy meetings, an active involvement she would continue until the early 1960s.[5] She served on sub-committees considering appropriate action for issues that the council identified as being of especial and growing concern in a Belfast that, although it was now the capital of the new Northern Ireland state, was not only struggling to cope with the privations of the post-war economic slump but also endured a cycle of communal and sectarian violence that saw over 400 fatalities in the early years of the 1920s.[6]

In the prolonged period of economic depression between the world wars, the work of the Belfast Council of Social Welfare occupied an increasing proportion of Emma's time. In 1933 she was elected Honorary Secretary, a post she held until 1953.[7] Her special interests included the provision of suitable housing, an area in which Belfast Corporation proved itself to be notoriously deficient. She was the principal force behind the establishment of what was called an After-Care committee. It was concerned by, for instance, improving the prospects of women emerging from hospital, either as patients or as new mothers, who were expected to resume fully and immediately their household duties. It was entirely in keeping with this family tradition of public service, therefore, that Emma accepted the post of Commandant of the VAD unit based at Stranmillis Military Hospital, on the site of Stranmillis Training College, whose student teachers had been relocated to Fawcett's Hotel in Portrush, Co. Antrim.[8]

First year Stranmillis students studying in Portrush May 1941.

A watercolour sketch of the Blue Pool, Portrush, painted by trainee teacher J.D. Cameron as part of his studies in Portrush during April 1940.

[4] Deirdre Heenan and Derek Birrell, *Social Policy in Northern Ireland: Conflict and Change* (Bristol, 2011), p.13

[5] PRONI, D2086/AA/3 extract from *The Northern Whig* 9 February 1923 'Social welfare. The Work of the Council in Ulster'.

[6] Jonathan Bardon, *A History of Ulster* (Belfast, 1992), p.494 says that 'between July 1920 and July 1922 the death toll in the six counties [of the new state] was 557' of which 416 were in Belfast.

[7] PRONI, D2086/AA/3. The meeting of the Executive Committee 21 November 1933 records her acceptance of the post.

[8] George Beal and Eamon Phoenix, *Stran. Stranmillis College 1922–1998. An Illustrated History* (Belfast, 1998), p.21 observe that 'At the opening of hostilities in September 1939 the College site and buildings were required by the military as a hospital and the training college was evacuated to a hotel in Portrush on the north Antrim coast.'

4

'I … rather reluctantly agreed as I had put my name down at the beginning of the war to serve if called on'.[9]

Preparations for war

Emma's early entries in the diary serve as a useful guide to how the public in Northern Ireland responded to the prospect of war during the nervous summer months of 1939 and then the news in early September that Britain was finally at war. The lack of preparedness of the Northern Ireland government in the years immediately before and even in the early days of the war has been well documented, not least by Brian Barton who pulls no punches, confirming that although 'experts had informed Stormont ministers in early 1939 that Belfast was a likely Luftwaffe target, few steps were taken to prepare it for war'.[10] As for Belfast itself, 'the city's passive defences were equally ill-prepared'. [11] Nothing in Emma's diary entries runs counter to this diagnosis of lethargic preparation for modern warfare that would, for the first time, involve civilian populations on a wide scale.

The radio and public information

One of the issues that her diary entries highlight is the role played by radio broadcasts put out by the BBC in providing general information at a time when, inevitably, it became more controlled. It is clear that she listens intently to 'the wireless', commenting that 'Churchill's voice on the wireless inspired confidence and one felt that men could follow such a leader'; likewise King George VI's 'simple but inspiring speech' with 'hardly a trace of his usual stammer'. Her diary reflects the mounting concern and apprehension as the news came through that, one by one, western European countries succumbed to German invading forces. Emma had spent a year as a governess in Germany shortly before the outbreak of the First World War. When she found the BBC broadcasts 'disappointing, slight, frivolous programmes, uninspired, give one a feeling they are fiddling while Rome burns', she was therefore able to tune in on long wave radio to broadcasts from France and Germany. The sense of mounting drama is, if anything, increased by her description of listening to speeches by Goebbels, Goering and Hitler, their 'raucous, thick, coarse voices, hurling invective, threats, curses at the allies'.

---

[9] PRONI, D2109/18/9 p.30

[10] Brian Barton, *The Belfast Blitz. The City in the War Years* (Belfast, 2015), p.32.

[11] Barton *op cit* p.33

Public reaction to the war

Emma was appointed Commandant in early March 1940.[12] Until then her diary reflects not only her own views on the early days of the war, and how it compared with her experience of 1914 but she also comments on how other people have reacted, initially to the threat and then to the early impact of the war. In this regard she echoes some of the comments made by Moya Woodside, a correspondent in Northern Ireland of the Mass Observation Archive established shortly before the war by Tom Harrisson, specifically with a view of noting the reactions of the public in the United Kingdom to events as they were happening at home, and elsewhere. Emma's observations relate generally to public morale: 'I have never heard one who thought we were going to lose the war'. It also throws some light on the circumstances of Northern Ireland. Conscription was not introduced, which meets with her approval and on occasion she comments on the extent to which rationing privations appear to be not quite as severe as they were in Great Britain. Even when 'such things as marmalade and all foreign fruit, bananas, oranges etc. became unattainable … the standard of food remained wonderfully good'.

Her VAD unit was based at Stranmillis Training College which had been transformed into a military hospital. It was within walking distance of the Duffin family home at Mount Pleasant on Stranmillis Road and Emma did indeed live at home in the first instance. She was not given much, if any, information about her duties prior to taking up the post. As it turned out, it was largely an administrative post, superintending the VAD nurses who were in her charge. As she comments 'there was hardly anything to do' and contents herself with the observation that it was because she and her senior colleague were good administrators. Much of her time is spent initially on getting to grips with the broad range of 'AFs and ACIs (Army Forms and Army Council Instructions)' and she occasionally gives vent to her frustration with military bureaucracy: 'Every difficulty was put in the way. I said bitterly later that the fighting in France [in the First World War] was nothing to the fighting that went on to get anything done in the army'.

Training at Aldershot

Immediately on taking up her duties at Stranmillis Emma spent two weeks furthering her training at the main army base at Aldershot in

---

[12] PRONI D2109/20/5, 'Part 1 Order. No. 58 6.3.40 … VAD Commandant Miss Duffin reported for duty at Military Hospital, Stranmillis w.e.f. 5.3.40'

6

Hampshire where she learned more about the administrative, even bureaucratic, nature of her position and her role in charge of the nurses. She concluded that 'one of the chief jobs of the Commandant was filling in passes for them. These passes seemed to me ridiculously elaborate'. Her time at Aldershot appears to have been enlightening only to the extent of alerting her to the significant relaxation of conditions of service of VAD nurses compared with those under which VAD nurses served in the First World War. Modern nurses were, she concluded, 'as was to be expected of this generation, much more independent than we had been'.

Stranmillis Military Hospital

On return to Belfast her administrative tasks and struggles with army bureaucracy were resumed. She was particularly mindful of ensuring that the nurses in her care were suitably provided for though, as she ruefully observed, 'it was extraordinary how one had to struggle for the most obvious necessities'. She describes a few desultory evacuation and fire drills that were practised at Stranmillis. Emma refers to the aerial raids by Luftwaffe bombers on cities in England that had begun in September 1940 but, as was apparent elsewhere in Northern Ireland and particularly at government level, there appeared to be no general concern. However, from June 1940 when Germany had invaded France, Belfast was now more readily within striking distance of German bombers: 'we had a few air raid warnings and orders and counter orders regarding them'. Nonetheless, the city, as she remarks, 'had been singularly free from air raid warnings… until April 1941'. It was all about to change dramatically.

Easter 1941 Blitz

'On Tuesday April 15 [19]41 I was awakened by the sirens at 10.45' (which happened to be Easter Tuesday) is Emma's opening observation of what would turn out to be a remarkable testimony to the most traumatic night in the history of the city. She describes the sounds of the bombs which fell throughout the long night, mainly on the northern part of the city. The Stranmillis military hospital 'got few casualties' but when Emma checked up on her other area of responsibility, the Donegall Road military hospital, she found that the VAD nurses had become upset by the lorries bearing dead bodies to the mortuary. It continues to remain a mystery why, given that Belfast was a recognised target because of its industrial and shipbuilding output, it was residential areas, particularly in the north of the city, that took the full brunt of the German aerial attack. However, the outcome was that close on eight hundred inhabitants were

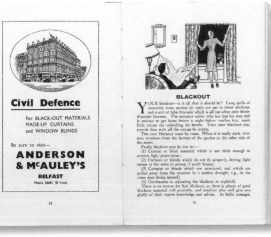

PRONI D2003/F/7

killed that night, in all likelihood more in one night than in any other UK city apart from London.[13]

It was only two days later, when she undertook to travel to the top of Oldpark Road where she was scheduled to give one of a series of first aid talks to the Women's Voluntary Service, that the extent of the damage inflicted became fully apparent.[14] Her itinerary from the city centre took her, by one means or another, through some of the most badly affected areas. Emma found her way, quite intrepidly, through the ruined streets, from Royal Avenue to Carlisle Circus and past the Mater Infirmorum hospital on Crumlin Road 'where many victims had been taken'. Her route on foot from the city centre would quite possibly have taken her into Unity Street, the scene of a devastating direct hit on an Air Raid Precaution post in which twelve people were killed outright.[15] Continuing up the Crumlin Road she describes 'little side streets in ruins, houses reduced to rubble' and 'a street shelter that had received a direct hit'. It says much about her determined nature that Emma continued on what must have been a daunting itinerary across the city.

In the course of her weary way back 'there were no trams … buses were so crowded there was no hope of a seat', she witnessed 'demolition squads and military digging frantically' and met 'everywhere … people with parcels or suitcases struggling to get away. Who could blame them?'. Travelling on foot as she did, she encountered displaced and bombed-out victims including 'a friendly little person who had been a VAD in the last war [who] had come to look for a friend but found her gone'.

Undaunted, and in spite of her harrowing journey through such scenes of devastation, the following day, the third after the Blitz, she returned to the northern part of the city, that which had been most seriously damaged, to look in on 'the nurses' home in Frederick Street … and as I had been on

---

[13] Barton, *op. cit.*, p.268 confirms 'that approximately 745 civilians died in Belfast as a result of the Easter Tuesday raid'. An unknown number of armed forces fatalities should be added to this.

[14] Barton, *op. cit.*, p.469 says that during the 2 raids, 15–16 April and 4–5 May, 'over 380 bombers participated and 440 tons of high explosives were dropped, along with 125,000 incendiary bombs.'

[15] Barton *op. cit.*, p.169 lists the names of seven individuals killed at the Unity Street post. Their ages range from John McKenna aged 15, an ARP messenger, to Michael Farrelly aged 26, the group warden.

8

the committee in pre-war days I thought I would go round and inquire for the Matron'. The patients had been moved to nearby Clifton House, the oldest-established charity in Belfast.[16]

She also makes an insightful observation on the evacuees, saying that 'The usual tales were told of the incredible dirt of the people: of children crawling with lice, not even house-trained … a terrible indictment of our way of life'. This echoed comments of Moya Woodside in the record she was making elsewhere in Ulster for the Mass Observation Archive of the impact the lifestyle of the evacuees from Belfast had made on the provincial households where they had been billeted. It was observations such as these in towns and cities throughout war-torn England that had created the conditions for the inquiry conducted by William Beveridge, whose report in December 1942, recommending that a comprehensive social care system should become more of a state responsibility, created something of a template for the post-war welfare state.[17]

St George's Market Morgue

Exacting as all this was, Emma's day spent on duty at St George's Market on the Saturday after the Blitz, proved to be as challenging as anything she had yet encountered. Responding to a request from her younger sister Molly, she reported for duty to what was the most spacious repository where unidentified bodies of bomb victims could be laid out, this with a view to helping their positive identification. There she accompanied relatives looking for loved ones. In the course of this macabre search, they had to look into coffins only generally marked 'young girl dark hair' or 'fair girl wearing necklace'. The ghastliness was if anything made all the greater by her finding a young girl 'of about 7 or 8 sitting on a chair waiting for her mother. How anyone could have allowed a child to enter that Hall of Death I do not know'. She compared this experience to her association with dead bodies in the First World War where 'I had seen many dead, but they had died in hospital beds, their eyes had been reverently closed, their hands crossed on their breasts; death had been glossed over, made decent …. Here it was grotesque, repulsive, horrible … Death should be dignified, peaceful. Hitler had made even death grotesque'.

---

[16] The Belfast Charitable Society, in Clifton Street, was first built in the 1770s and remains one of the city's longest-surviving buildings.

[17] Inter-Departmental committee on Social Insurance and Allied Services. (1942) *Social Insurance and Allied Services* [the Beveridge Report], (Cmd. 6404), (London: HMSO).

Second aerial raid

The second major air raid, on Sunday 4 May, was equally damaging: this time the Luftwaffe did find their industrial targets, to the extent that 'only' 199 people were killed during the raid. As she listened to 'the thuds of the bombs' throughout that long night Emma reflected somewhat resignedly on her experience of the April raid: 'having seen those pathetic streets smashed to dust, those distorted bodies, the horror was brought home to me more but, I'm glad to say, though I felt horrified I did not feel fear'. But even as she returned in the early morning light to her quarters when the all-clear was given, Emma was looking to a brighter future: 'The grass was strewn with blackened and charred papers. There was a sheet from a child's essay book. On top of the page I read '"The end of the world". It seemed appropriate. It was the end of the world as we knew it'. And then, as if somehow recognising the value of war as an agent for bringing about social, even political, change, she adds 'Let us hope it will be the beginning of a better one'.

Post-Blitz Changes

Emma resumed her 'normal' duties as VAD Commandant at Stranmillis Military Hospital, returning to the daily, largely administrative, routine of superintending the VAD nurses in her charge. She found that not only was the army's bureaucratic inflexibility as frustrating as before but, unfortunately for her, her relationship with the recently-appointed matron continued to be a source of disappointment. Matters came to a head when Emma felt that she and her VADs had been misled over the arrangements they had been making for an end of year dance, perhaps their only major social engagement of the year and an occasion, as Emma knew well from her First World War experience, which was a focal point of the nurses' social year. After this disagreeable episode, Emma's diary entries dry up quite abruptly.

Postscript

Later, in 1967, she observes that she couldn't quite recollect why she had stopped keeping the diary, putting it down to being 'too busy I suppose'. However, the likelihood is that, although things must have looked up when she found that Matron was transferred to Gilford, 'something of a come-down for her', it was almost certainly the changes proposed in the Elliott Report affecting the status of VADs and specifically the rank of Commandant, Emma's rank, that betokened the beginning of the end of her Second World War contribution.[18] The report recommended that VAD nurses be assimilated into the Auxiliary Territorial Service. Not only would they lose their prized 'volunteer' status, but, as the report put it, 'VAD personnel shall ... in the same manner as members of the ATS be subject to military law and be enrolled into the women's forces ... at present VAD personnel serving with the Army are only to a limited degree subject to military law as civilians'. The report's further justification of these thoroughgoing changes was hardly a worthy reflection on the value of the contribution of thousands of VAD units in both wars: 'The Army Council case for merger was twofold...it would enable the best use to be made of man and woman power. Many VAD members were people of high intelligence and capacity and it was felt that their gifts fitted them for something considerably better'. On top of that the rank of Commandant was recommended to be disbanded entirely.

Alarmed as much by the loss of her VAD charges' status as her own, Emma was provoked to write in June 1943, over a year after she had stopped her diary entries, to Lady Mountbatten, Superintendent-in-Chief of the St John Ambulance Brigade. Her principal worries related to the anomalies of incorporating the VADs into the ATS, 'Many of the VADs have had three or four years' experience yet, as I understand it, they are now to hold the same rank as the ATS do after six weeks, namely "Nursing Orderlies".' She also feared for discipline and respect on the wards: 'The patients call them by their first names, treat them with familiarity and no respect and they share a mess with the hospital male orderlies ... in my opinion it will inevitably lead to lack of discipline in the wards'. Her closing affirmation of loyalty cannot disguise her deep sense of disappointment: 'Needless to say I will loyally abide by the committee's decision and do my best to see my VADs accept its ruling. I make no secret of the fact that I anticipate resentment and dismay when they learn of it'.[19]

Emma was moved to the military hospital located at Bangor and, although she was able to live with her sister in Holywood rather than tolerate the comparatively inhospitable living quarters she was offered, it nonetheless

---

[18] War Office. (1943) *Report of the Committee on Voluntary Aid Detachments, The Elliott Committee*, (Cmd. 6448), (London: HMSO). Its terms of reference were 'to consider the scope and method of employment of mobile VADs by, and their relationship to, the Services.'

[19] PRONI, D2109/20/5, 3 June 1943, letter from 'Commandant Emma S. Duffin to The Lady Louis Mountbatten, Lady Superintendent, St John Ambulance Brigade'.

left her with something of a sour taste in her mouth, as her sad postscript notes: 'I look back at my time at Bangor with a feeling of disgust'. She had undergone the full range of wartime privations, all of which she would have stoically shrugged off. In this context, and even though Emma herself would have subscribed to the philosophy 'there's a war on, you know', it does seem singularly inappropriate and unfair that this civilian volunteer who, initially as a young woman and then, latterly as an experienced social administrator, had rallied to the cause in two world wars, at home and abroad, could not have been left with a more deserving and fonder recollection of a service that was by any standards above and beyond the call of duty.

Post 1945

Emma had continued to serve throughout the war as Honorary Secretary of the Belfast Council of Social Welfare. Before the war, she had been the main instigator of an After-Care committee, concerned to provide services for children and mothers on their immediate discharge from hospital. With the gradual introduction post-1948 in Northern Ireland of a statutory welfare system she became concerned to ensure that the new structures incorporated the main characteristics of the After-Care committee. She was part of a delegation to the Ministry of Home Affairs which focused specifically on child care. She was also involved in such matters as the raising of money in the wake of the Princess Victoria sinking disaster in 1953.[20] Although she attained the age of seventy later that year it must have come as something of a surprise to the Belfast Council of Social Welfare that such a mainspring of its activities should announce her resignation from the post of Honorary Secretary.[21] Emma stayed on the committee, however, until the early 1960s. Her public service was recognised not only by the warm note of appreciation in the B.C.S.W. minutes but also, the following year, by the award in 1954 of an Honorary Master of the Arts by Queen's University of Belfast. She was presented for the award by Professor E. Estyn Evans, the distinguished historical geographer and ethnographer. His encomium observed that 'years ago the University honoured Miss Ruth Duffin, distinguished first Warden of Riddel Hall. It must be rare, short of Royalty, for two sisters to become

[20] PRONI, D2086/AA/5.

[21] PRONI, D2086/AA/5. Executive Committee meeting 5 November 1953, 'The Chairman reported that Miss Duffin had found it necessary to tender her resignation from the Honorary Secretaryship which she had held for 20 years'.

Cover and illustration designed by Emma Duffin for her sister Ruth's children's book, *The Fairy Cup*

honorary graduates of the same university but the Duffin family was little short of Royalty … in the tradition of public service it had maintained through the generations.' He continued: 'Miss Duffin showed a … capacity for the practical application of her ideas. It was she who, after having seen and proved the need for after-care services, initiated the Belfast Hospitals' After-Care Committee. In 1937, when the Council's housing scheme was launched it was Miss Duffin who fought masculine prejudice by insisting that the houses should have convenient kitchens as well as pleasing facades'.[22]

Diary as witness

Emma Duffin's Second World War diary differs from those she had kept while serving in the First World War in a number of respects. It was entered up more regularly, principally because her circumstances allowed access to pen and paper more easily than had been the case while she had been on duty in either Alexandria or in Le Havre. Having discontinued regular entries towards the end of 1942, she only completes her story as late as 1967 when, interestingly, she feels freer than was the case a generation earlier to raise issues, such as pregnancy among the nurses and her own disenchantment with the changes in regulations that effectively rendered her position redundant.

Another major difference is that during the First World War she rarely if ever questioned how it was being conducted. This diary, on the other hand, is altogether more opinionated, mainly arising from her greater maturity and increasing frustration with army procedures and, to a certain extent, on the position she held, as a VAD Commandant with responsibility for up to one hundred nurses.

Additionally, the diary serves to record from an individual's perspective the impact of modern warfare, specifically aerial bombardments, on a civilian population. The extent to which the Second World War involved civilians to a previously unknown degree (not until 1943 did the number of military casualties outnumber civilian) is brought home, in more senses than one, by Emma's diary observations that, sensitively and graphically, as befitted a book illustrator, describe one of the most traumatic events in Belfast's history.[23]

---

[22] D2109/20/5 contains the text of Prof. E. Estyn Evans' address when presenting Emma Duffin for an Honorary M.A. at Queen's University Belfast July 1954.

[23] Emma designed and illustrated greetings and Christmas cards and books, including children's books by her sister Ruth (*The Fairy Cup* and *Handy Andy and the Wee House*) and volumes of poetry by her sisters, *The Secret Hill* (1913) by Ruth and *Escape. Poems* (1929) by Ruth and Celia Duffin.

THE QUEEN'S UNIVERSITY OF BELFAST

FACULTY OF ARTS

TELEPHONE:
BELFAST 21821

SUMMER GRADUATION CEREMONY JULY 7, 1954.

Emma Sylvia Duffin

Eleven years ago the University honoured Miss Ruth Duffin, the distinguished first warden of Riddel Hall. Today it is my pleasure to present another gracious member of that gifted family. It must be rare, short of Royalty, for two sisters to become honorary graduates of the same University, but the Duffin family is little short of Royalty in its memories and in the tradition of public service which it has maintained through the generations. The proud mother of these sisters, who in this hallowed month of July becomes a centenarian, is in touch, at one remove, with the storied 1690's. She was brought up by a grandmother whose father, mirabile dictu was born in the seventeenth century.

For many decades the family has stood for liberal ideas and for liberal service to the community. It might indeed be said that the link of the Duffins with voluntary social work goes back to Adam, for Adam Duffin was the first Vice-Chairman of the Belfast Charity Organisation, which was to become the Belfast Council of Social Welfare. For twenty years Miss Emma Duffin was the honorary secretary and moving spirit of the Council.

In all her activities Miss Duffin shows a rare combination of quick perception and warm human sympathies with a capacity for the practical application of her ideas. It was she who, having seen and proved the need for after-care services, initiated the Belfast Hospitals' After-Care Committee. In 1937, when the Councils' Housing Scheme was launched, it was Miss Duffin who fought masculine prejudice by insisting that the houses should have convenient kitchens as well as pleasing façades.

Miss Duffin's fighting qualities were already in evidence in the 1914-18 War, when she served with the V.A.D. in Egypt and France, and was mentioned in Despatches. During the Second World War she was V.A.D. Commandant of Stranmillis Military Hospital.

N.B.
Adam
Duffin
L.L.D.
Hon-Causa
1882.

Emma Duffin was presented by Prof. E. Estyn Evans for the award of Honorary Master of the Arts at Queen's University, Belfast, July 1954.

THE QUEEN'S UNIVERSITY OF BELFAST

FACULTY OF ARTS

TELEPHONE:
BELFAST 21821

2.

Her interest in the care and education of children has shown itself in many ways: in sponsoring schemes for the teaching of young patients in the City Hospitals; in bringing colour and beauty into Public Elementary Schools through the Schools Pictures Committee; and not least in writing and illustrating several charming childrens' books. Nothing could more clearly demonstrate the Duffin quality of holding in balance the gifts of mind and manner, heart and hand.

Chancellor of the University, my Lord, I present to you EMMA SYLVIA DUFFIN for the degree of Master of Arts, honoris causa.

E. Estyn Evans.

Extract from a History of the BELFAST COUNCIL OF SOCIAL WELFARE. -
by Alex. Macbeath.

Miss EMMA DUFFIN, Hon. Secretary from 1933 to 1953 and now a Vice-President, a woman who combined modesty and gentleness and kindness with great strength of character and quiet efficiency."

"Others who should be mentioned as specially active in the service of the society were Mr and Mrs ADAM DUFFIN, the former first as Vice-Chairman of Council and later as Vice-President."

During the 1914-1918 war I kept a diary, and though it was not written from day to day it was written while all the events were freshly in my mind & may some day be of interest. It is unlikely that in this war I will be able to take any active part, but having served as a V.A.D. in a military hospital during the last, I have, as we have been asked to do, registered again for nursing service at a First Aid Post, but, being 25 years older would only be able to work for short spells. On this account this diary will probably be less interesting and I may later decide that it is not worth keeping. But I will begin by recording some of one's impressions before & since the outbreak of war.

Ever since the Czecho-Slovakian crisis I thought everyone felt it was only a matter of time before another one, & that the danger was only averted, not for the time. Personally I felt, & I know many others did, that Chamberlain had been fooled by Hitler, that the little scrap of paper he waved triumphantly was worthless & that his words 'Peace in our time', only showed that he had been easily duped by Hitler. I admired him for his peace efforts, but repelled his complacency, and when I read the terms to the Czechs with which we had bought our temporary peace I was filled with shame, as were thousands of

1 The Phoney War

Emma Duffin had served as a VAD nurse in the First World War and she very soon after wrote up a journal of her experiences. As the war clouds gathered over Europe in the late summer of 1939, she resumed her diary. Although her expectation that 'It is unlikely that in this war I will be able to take any active part' was reversed when she was appointed Commandant of a VAD unit, the early entries in her diary reflect the skills as a chronicler of wartime events she had displayed twenty-five years earlier.

In addition to her grasp of the fast-moving political events that preceded the United Kingdom's declaration of war on Germany on 3 September 1939, Emma displays an awareness of the potential for evil that was unfolding. Her criticism of Prime Minister Neville Chamberlain – 'had he ever read *Mein Kampf*?' – suggests that she herself, a fluent German speaker, was acutely aware of its message even if she had not read it herself. This familiarity with the German language adds a frisson to her account of listening for news to the 'wireless', as she calls it. She describes the family (they all spoke the language, having been tutored by German governesses) gathering round in the evening to listen in to broadcasts from Nazi Germany. Indeed, one of the striking features of her and, no doubt, many others' family life was the extent to which the population depended on the radio for information.

Emma's other early observations also include some slightly dismissive but, as it turned out, accurate views on the general preparedness for war locally, including air raid precautions and the evacuation process, reflecting the unspoken assumption that 'it couldn't happen here'. Her frustration with the 'phoney' war – 'this was a strange war, this one, that started so slowly. When, we asked ourselves, is our army going to take part?' – would soon change, as she took up a role, Commandant of the VAD unit based at Stranmillis Military Hospital, she had not expected and which would, within a year, pitch her into the midst of the cataclysmic air raids on the city.

facing
The first of the 138 closely-written pages in Emma's Second World War diary.
PRONI D2109/18/9

16   *diary pages 1–24*   During the 1914–18 war I kept a diary and though it was not written from day to day it was written while all the events were fresh in my mind and may some day be of interest.[24] It is unlikely that in this war I will be able to take any active part but having served as a V.A.D. in a military hospital during the last war I have, as we all have been asked to do, registered again for nursing service at a First Aid Post but, being 25 years older, would only be able to work for short spells. On this account this diary will probably be less interesting and I may later decide that it is not worth keeping, but I will begin by recording some of our impressions before and on the outbreak of war.[25]

Ever since the Czecho-Slovakian crisis I think everyone felt it was only a matter of time before another one and that the danger was only averted for the time. Personally I felt, and I know many others did, that Chamberlain had been fooled by Hitler, that the little scrap of paper he waved triumphantly was worthless and that his words 'peace in our time' only showed that he had been easily duped by Hitler.[26] I admired him for his peace efforts but regretted his complacency and when I heard the terms to the Czechs, with which we had bought our 'temporary' peace, I was filled with alarm, as were thousands of others. We had bought peace, and a temporary one at that, by sacrificing the Czechs. It is argued that there was no other course open as we were totally unprepared but what right had we to be unprepared when we had guaranteed Czechoslovakia? The Germans had made no secret of their re-arming. It was obvious to the man in the street that they were doing it for a purpose. Why then did the politicians not recognize that fact or, if they did, ignore it? I consider they laid themselves open to blame for in their hands lay the safety of the country. Disarmament is a fine thing to aim for but can only be done if all the countries disarm. For England and France to disarm with the knowledge that Germany was re-arming seemed to the uninitiated criminal folly. If Germany could not be prevented from re-arming then we should have marched step-by-step with her; for every big gun she made France and England should have built one, for every aeroplane built in Germany there should have been one built in France, in England. But who can fathom the minds of politicians? I must say when Chamberlain

---

[24] There are five of Emma Duffin's First World War diaries in PRONI, D2109/18/4, 5A, 5B, 6 and 7.

[25] Emma Duffin kept one Second World War diary, here transcribed. PRONI, D2109/18/9.

[26] 'Peace in our time' is attributed to Prime Minister Neville Chamberlain, 30 September 1938, on return to England following talks with Adolf Hitler in Munich aimed at averting war.

confessed to liking Hitler and said when Hitler declared he had no further territorial aspirations in Europe, that he believed him, I felt angry at such folly. A Prime Minister should be a better judge of character. He has no right to be so duped or he is not fit to lead his people. Had he ever read 'Mein Kampf'? Had he not heard of the 'Putsch'?[27] Did he not know how the Jews had been treated? Why did he like and believe Hitler? I felt sorry for him later, disillusioned, all his hopes of keeping the peace he had struggled for gone. But there was just a slightly irritating touch of complacency, no admission that he had been mistaken in his policy, in his speeches. That rather alienated my sympathy.

Will's Cigarette Card album
of Air Raid Precautions

NIWM Collection

Invet Museum Collection
of St John Ambulance Memorabilia

A roundel
for easy identification
of gases and appropriate
treatment

All the winter before the war I had attended A.R.P. classes and in the spring had gone down in the evenings to fit people with gas masks. Time will show if these precautions were as futile as they seemed. It was annoying to turn out in the cold, dark winter nights, to listen to lectures on mustard gas when we felt that the decontamination as described would be impossible to carry out. It was foolish to tell people they must strip their walls, re-paper them three times and then do them with water glass or that all the beams under their roofs should be painted with lime. We knew nobody could or would attempt to carry out these instructions! We learnt the names and smell of the gases, sniffed them knowingly from

[27] *Mein Kampf (My Struggle)* is a two-volume autobiographical manifesto by Adolf Hitler, published 1925–26, partly written in jail following his part in the failed 1923 Putsch ('push', meaning an attempted overthrow).

glass tubes and finally took the exams and were given an A.R.P. badge. The fitting [of] the gas masks was tiring but had its amusing side. Frightened old people, giggling girls, shy boys lined up to be fitted and departed with their masks in frail and inadequate boxes. We were all told to take them everywhere but I'm afraid we left them in Belfast when we went to Newcastle and our three little nieces and their mother arrived without them.[28]

NIWM Collection

We had taken *Shimna*, a nice shabby old house with a beautiful garden sloping down to the river with Slieve Donard for a background.[29] Win Plumpton was staying and came with us.[30] We knew of course that the clouds were gathering but we had got accustomed to crisises [sic] and in the peaceful atmosphere of Newcastle it was difficult to realize that the world was on the edge of an abyss. After Win left, Dorfy and the

[28] Emma's observations on the paucity of Belfast's defences are borne out by James Doherty in *Post 381: The Memoirs of a Belfast Air Raid Warden* (Belfast, 1989) in which he recounts his experiences as an Air Raid Protection warden in north Belfast and by Brian Barton, *The Belfast Blitz. The City in the War Years.* (Belfast, 2015) pp.38-42.

[29] 'Shimna' is now Shimna Integrated College. Slieve Donard is one of Northern Ireland's highest mountains, in the Mourne range, picturesquely situated near Newcastle, south County Down.

[30] Emma had befriended Winifred Plumpton when they served together as Voluntary Aid Detachment nurses in France in the First World War.

children arrived.[31] I and some of us returned to Belfast to make room for them. I had been seedy and was leading a lazy life. Dorfy, always dramatic, told us she had a friend at the Admiralty who would send her what she called a 'code' telegram, 'Mary ill return'! We all rather giggled over this, I'm afraid. She went to pay visits and later Mother and I joined the children and other members of the family at Newcastle.

The weather was beautiful. We sat in the sun, gazed at the mountains and tried not to think of the possibilities of war which like a dark shadow loomed nearer each day. Jack and Mary Barrett and their two girls and boy were there and Tom and Iris Sinclair and their youngest boy. Tom, ever optimistic, was sure there would be no war; Hitler would climb down. Iris fretted and wanted to go home. Aug 22. Suddenly D., Brian and Dorfy arrived unexpectedly about 12 o'clock, Dorfy wild with excitement. She had had her code telegram!! It later transpired she had in reality rung up her friend who had advised her return. She rushed upstairs and began to pack the children's clothes as if the Germans were at her heels. In half an hour or less they were all packed into the motor and had departed, regardless of the fact that the boat did not go till 9.15pm. We were whirled off our feet and wondered vaguely afterwards why they had brought a chauffeur and Brian as D. generally drove and it meant that they were packed like herrings in a barrel on the way back. People like to do things abnormally in crises, even if unnecessarily. It is all part of the game! Well, the children had gone. We had taken the house for them and engaged extra maids. It was all most annoying but a small matter compared with what was coming.

Tom and Iris came round. Some English people were leaving the hotel. 'Panic mongers' said Tom. 'No need to go' Iris fretted. She was not well and the two eldest boys were in the army and John was agape to go. No wonder she was nervous. Three days later they came to say goodbye. War loomed nearer and ever nearer. We had not brought our wireless and the newspapers came late every day. There were the usual rumours. Then came the news the Germans had attacked Poland and the brave Poles had defied them.[32] To them goes the honour of being the first

---

[31] *Dorfy* was the pet name of Emma's sister-in-law, Dorothy, whose husband Major Terence Duffin MC had died in 1936. Emma also had a sister Dorothy, hence the convention of a nickname.

[32] Germany attacked Poland on 1 September 1939, leading directly to Britain's declaration of war on 3 September.

people to stand up to Hitler and his bullies and God knows they were to pay that honour dearly.

Sep 1st came Chamberlain's grave warning to the Germans to withdraw but we all realized that it was in vain. No words would stop the beast of Nazism. Poland was doomed, France and England were pledged. There could be no second Munich if our country wished to avoid being branded for ever with dishonour. There was no turning back. We all knew it was inevitable. I never heard a dissentient voice nor anyone suggest we could hold back. Everyone who remembered 1914 and the invasion of Belgium and how we held our breath lest the politicians should decide not to go to war felt the same again. We had seen the horrors of war. We would have given everything we possessed to avert it, save honour but it wasn't to be. We must fight and sacrifice our men and our family once again.

On Sunday 3rd Mr Chamberlain announced that we were at war with Germany. We had brought our wireless down and we listened to his grave words and to the Liberal and Opposition leaders. Thank God we were at one. All parties were united. There had been talk of a railway strike. It was called off. There was a stiffer fight ahead. In the afternoon we heard France had declared war. The next day Beth and I went up to town to measure windows and order A.R.P. cloth. I trekked round the shops. There was none to be had. It was sold out.

Belfast Telegraph headline announcing the 'formal declaration of hostilities' in its 'Special' (Sunday) edition 3 September 1939.

'S Belfast Telegraph

THIRD SPECIAL

70th YEAR   [REGISTERED AT THE G.P.O. AS A NEWSPAPER]   SUNDAY, SEPTEMBER 3, 1939.   [THREE-HALFPENCE]

BRITAIN AND FRANCE AT WAR WITH GERMANY

FORMAL DECLARATION OF HOSTILITIES

The following official communique was issued from 10 Downing Street: On September 1 His Majesty's Ambassador in Berlin was instructed to inform the German Government that unless they were prepared to give His Majesty's Government satisfactory assurances that the German Government would suspend any aggressive action against Poland and were prepared promptly to withdraw their forces from Polish territory, His Majesty's Government would without hesitation fulfil its obligations to Poland.

At nine this morning His Majesty's Ambassador in Berlin informed the German Government that unless not later than 11 a.m. to-day (British Summer Time), satisfactory assurances to the above effect had been given and had reached His Majesty's Government in London a state of war would exist between the countries from that hour.

Shortly after eleven the Prime Minister said "This country is at war with Germany."

France delivered a final ultimatum to Germany demanding that German troops withdraw from Poland. The ultimatum expires at five p.m. (B.S.T.).

The British and French Ambassadors formally bade goodbye to von Ribbentrop.

PREMIER'S STATEMENT | **HISTORIC SUNDAY PARLIAMENT** | **THEATRES TO CLOSE**

"LONG STRUGGLE TO WIN" | *Stresses The Nation's Oneness* | SPORTS GATHERINGS TO CEASE

Just before we declared war, all the children from London, Glasgow, Liverpool and all towns in danger zones were evacuated. It may be worth recording for the future how it was organised. It had I think all been managed on paper during the Czecho Slovakian crisis and long before they were evacuated people had been visited in country places and warned that they must be prepared to receive children of school age and younger children with their mothers in the event of evacuation being considered necessary. The billeting was arranged according to the number of rooms in the house and very little regard was taken of the suitability of the posts in regard to health, age or temperament. The old saying that an Englishman's home was his castle no longer held good. If the man in the area responsible for billeting the children settled you were to have a certain number, there was no immediate redress. No doubt the Government was faced with a truly enormous problem but Governments must be prepared to tackle enormous problems or admit defeat. And many obvious difficulties and dangers were ignored. As far as we heard at the time, no effort had been made to make any arrangements, other than billeting them on private homes, for filthy, diseased and depraved children from the worst slums of the big cities. How could such a scheme be a success? There were dress rehearsals for the evacuation and naturally that must have been a model of organization for one heard no hint of difficulties arising through failure in transport or any form of confusion or overlapping.[33]

On the wireless we were told that the evacuation was carried out without a hitch and a complacent, sentimental voice told us of the children's arrival at homes where they were received with open arms, of their delight in their new surroundings etc. One bewildered little boy, when asked if he knew where he was going replied 'No, but the King does'. We smiled rather grimly and thanked our stars that Belfast was [not] a so-called dangerous area. We might live to regret it but for the present we were grateful. We foresaw, as most women might have, the difficulties ahead and some stories came though of indignant householders who had had foisted on them children, crawling with lice, children who turned clean bedrooms into latrines, mothers who drank tonic wine and grumbled and

---

[33] John A. Oliver was a civil servant involved in organising what turned out to be the abortive evacuation of civilian families from Belfast in early July 1940. In *Working at Stormont* (Dublin, 1978) p. 67 he describes how a colleague penned a Lewis Carroll-esque ditty recounting how they had 'wept like anything to see such quantities of fleas, such lousy little Protestants, such nitty young RCs.'

22

Evacuee payment card.
Families hosting evacuees
could expect to receive
payment at post offices.

NWM Collection

who spent more money than their unwilling hosts could afford to do. The people who had received children were given an allowance of 8/- weekly but found many of the children had no change of underclothing and nightwear, leaking boots, inadequate clothes and even where the clothing was adequate their hostesses had to wash and mend and cook for them. Desperate situations need desperate remedies it is true, but I do not think that the Government had really properly thought out or foreseen the result of their high-handed if necessary action. One heard more grumbling and discontent on this subject than on any other. There was probably another side to the picture, too. Homesick, lonely children in homes where they were met with black looks and disagreeable words. Anxious, worried parents who did not know into what kind of homes their children had gone. It is hardly to be wondered at that before very long some began to drift back to their own homes.

Meanwhile the poor Poles were maintaining a desperate resistance. One heard of cavalry charges against the German heavily mechanized units. Of villages bombed unceasingly by the German air force. History will give an accurate account of it; to us, as the news nightly told on the wireless reached our ears it seemed like an appalling nightmare. Everything was against them. The driest summer for fifty years had made their marshes solid for the oppressor's tanks. The beautiful, clear, still nights made it easier for the aeroplanes to hit their objectives. I had lately read the life of Marie Curie, that wonderful Polish woman and patriot.[34] I was glad she had not lived to see her country smashed by the powers of wickedness. It seemed as if once again the hell hounds were unleashed and evil had once more got in the ascendancy.

Molly and I went to tea with Lady Mabel Annesley.[35] She told us that in the event of children being evacuated from Belfast she had promised to take a secondary school, Ashleigh House, about 80 children, at the Castle, but she added they were to bring their own teachers, cooks,

[34] Marie Curie, born in Warsaw in 1867, had died in France only a few years previously, in 1934, quite possibly from the after-effects of her experiments with radiation that advanced the treatment and understanding of cancer.

[35] Lady Mabel Marguerite Annesley (1881–1959) in addition to being the title-holder to the expansive Annesley estate in Castlewellan, Co. Down was a renowned wood-engraver and water-colour painter. These and her other interests are commemorated by an Ulster History Circle Blue Plaque in her name at the Arboretum of Castlewellan Forest Park House, Co. Down.

maids etc.[36] She showed us all the vegetables she had grown and was growing – masses of onions. I said she must be intending to feed them all Irish stew. She was exercised in her mind about the lighting as all her corridors were lit by sky lights. Fortunately, our old house, Shimna, had shutters in all the rooms or we would have had to go home.

NIWM Collection

Fuel was one of the essential commodities rationed throughout the war.

The weather was lovely. Molly and I took our tea and went out in the small car *Jane Austen* and picnicked by a mountain stream towards Annalong. How peaceful and beautiful it was! All the peace and beauty of the world to be shattered at the whim of an unbalanced man and a handful of scoundrels. The German people owe this world something for having let these people gain the ascendancy. We had meant to sell the little car at the end of the summer, but we heard petrol restrictions were coming in and nobody would want to buy cars. The announcement soon came out: we were to have 6 gal[lons] monthly for the Morris 10. The other we did not intend to use. The lighting restrictions for cars were also published and were very drastic. I felt I would never want to drive after dark.

Image in Emma's diary showing how car headlights were covered during the black-out

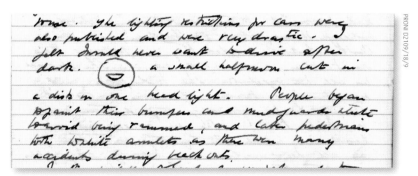

PRONI D2109/18/9

Poster showing how a car should be modified for the black-out

People began to paint their bumpers and mudguards white to avoid being rammed and later pedestrians took white armlets as there were many accidents during black-outs.

In the middle of September we returned to Belfast. After that our chief occupation was making curtains and shading lights and trying

Courtesy of the Royal Society for the Prevention of Accidents (RoSPA)

---

[36] Ashleigh House girls' school in south Belfast. Paula Beaumont and Hilary Maginnis, eds., *Princess Gardens School. A Goodly Heritage* (Belfast, 1993. pp. 393–6) describes the amalgamation in 1987 of Ashleigh House and Princess Gardens School, Upper Lisburn Road, Belfast. The name Hunterhouse College was adopted.

24

PRONI D2003/F/7

experiments. It was amazing the way light filtered out from the side of the blinds and over the tops of curtains. We sewed and sewed and fitted curtains, poles and wires and raked the town for rings and hooks. Fortunately in the meantime we had borrowed curtains from the Riddel Hall and hung them laboriously every night, inconvenient but effective.

Within a day or two of the declaration of war, the world had once more been horrified and shocked as it was by the sinking of the 'Lusitania' by the torpedoing of the 'Athenia', a vessel bound for America with only passengers, many of them Americans, on board.[37] She was sunk without warning and many people, including women and children, lost their lives. So once again the Germans started their ruthlessly cruel campaign of atrocities. What could one expect from the people who had struck a medal to celebrate the sinking of the 'Lusitania'? Not content with this act, they announced that England had done it as propaganda! What mentality? As in the last war, their stupid, unlikely statements were not able to convince the world but the Germans always seem to underestimate the intelligence of other people. They invented such stupid lies!

Every night we heard on the wireless of the sinking of ships but in most other cases the U-boat commanders seem to have given the crew some small chance of escape and some acted with real chivalry. It was depressing to hear of the sinking of ships and of the German success in Poland. Little news came over the wireless. We were not told when our troops reached France. At last news came of a daring raid on several German ports by the R.A.F. and later of flights over Germany and the dropping of propaganda papers. Then we heard that Winston Churchill was back at the Admiralty. The old sea dog had had to bide his time but his time had come. He sat where he had sat at the beginning of the last war. I remembered sitting at the Admiralty in his study while Dorothy, who had applied for a job, was carried off to do a shorthand and typing test before being established. I liked to think of him there again. Back too came Anthony Eden. They had warned the Government again and again what the results of the Munich Agreement would be and Mr Eden had left

---

[37] The *Athenia*, a Glasgow-built passenger liner, was the first ship to be sunk in the Second World War, in September 1939. There was a considerable number of Americans among the 128 people, passengers and crew, who drowned, leading Germany not to admit responsibility (until after the war) for fear of provoking American involvement in the war. The *Lusitania*, sunk off the west coast of Ireland in 1915, similarly had American passengers on board.

the Cabinet because of the policy of appeasement which he had seen would lead to war. Now, without recrimination or any hint of 'I told you so' he came back to help his country.[38]

The news continued to be very meagre. A new ministry, the Ministry of Information, was created. It had an enormous staff but they seemed to think their job was to suppress rather than give information. It is impossible to judge without full knowledge whether the criticism of it and the B.B.C was justified but to the un-informed there seemed room for criticism. Meagre news, dull unimaginative information came from both but I suspect they are both fully employed at propaganda. Probably the leaflets which the R.A.F. had strewn over Germany, even reaching Berlin unmolested, were from the Ministry of Information and the B.B.C. who are so busy giving propaganda in different languages to various countries that they appear to have little time to give any of value to their own. Still, we can't help feeling the home front should not be neglected and at any rate the news might be given at regular hours so that men need not sit half the day by the microphone to hear a bulletin that takes a couple of minutes to give out.

It seemed strange the way our part of the war started, so different from the last time. There seemed a reluctance to begin. The Germans obviously hoped, in spite of repeated warnings to the contrary, that if they could smash Poland quickly enough England and France would not come in. Bills were rushed through the house, conscription for boys from 19–22 being one of the more conspicuous. Food Control boards were appointed. Girls began to appear in the streets, self-conscious in new uniforms. The W.A.A.C. of the last war had become A.T.S. and the Fannies of 1914 were included.[39] Women were already driving lorries though there were still men out of work. Women were cooking for the troops and waiting in officers' messes where Tommies had cooked and waited. One couldn't help feeling a slight feeling of bitterness at the thought that our Children's Bill in N. Ireland had hung fire since

[38] Anthony Eden (1897–1977) had earlier resigned as Foreign Secretary in protest at Chamberlain's appeasement policy and was re-appointed in 1940, serving in that role until 1945.

[39] The Auxiliary Territorial Service (ATS) was the women's branch of the British army in the Second World War. Formed in 1938, the ATS had its roots in the Women's Auxiliary Army Corps (WAAC) formed initially in the First World War. The First Aid Nursing Yeomanry ('Fannies') served mainly as ambulance drivers in the First World War and had a more diverse role in the Second World War.

Women in the army in the Second World War, except nurses, joined the Auxiliary Territorial Service (ATS), formed in 1938

NIWM Collection

the English one was passed [in] 1932.[40] Then we heard of the care with which bills passed through Lords and Commons and how could we not reflect that money that was now being splashed recklessly out to kill our fellow men had not been forthcoming to save our unemployed from despair in the distressed areas. Now every little girl that could don a uniform drew a salary and a uniform allowance. Such are the ways of Government.

Rumours, as the inevitable accompaniments of war, were rife. Nothing would convince Doran, the gardener at *Shimna*, that Lord Londonderry was not interned in the Tower because of his former acquaintance with Ribbentrop.[41] Doran was very fierce on this subject and would have had him beheaded if it had lain in his power. We learnt that N. Ireland was not to have conscription. The danger of the I.R.A. and unwilling Catholic recruits was obviously the reason. There was a good deal of criticism but I think it was a wise decision.[42]

Bit by bit news sifted through. We heard with pride and later with astonishment that not only had the dominions offered their help to the Mother Country but that Arabs and Jews in Palestine were vying with each other in offering their services. We wondered what the Germans thought as they had been telling the world of British atrocities in Palestine. Then came the Indian princes offering money and even Ghandi calling

[40] Arising from her involvement in the work of the Belfast Council of Social Welfare, Emma had developed a particular interest in the need to provide greater statutory care for women and children.

[41] Charles Vane-Tempest-Stewart, the 7th Marquess of Londonderry, had been Minister for Education in the first Northern Ireland government and, latterly, Minister for Air in the Conservative government. He was convinced of the importance of maintaining links at all levels with Germany in a bid to reduce tension. As Peter Jupp's review of N.C. Fleming's *The Marquess of Londonderry. Aristocracy, Power and Politics in Britain and Ireland* (London, 2005) intimates, Londonderry 'set about a round of personal meetings with Ribbentrop, Goering and Hitler in an attempt to further good relations between the two countries'. This included a visit to the family home, Mount Stewart, near Newtownards, Co. Down, by the German ambassador, von Ribbentrop, giving rise to local fears of the sort voiced by the Duffin family gardener.

[42] Thomas Bartlett and Keith Jeffery, eds., *A Military History of Ireland* (Cambridge University Press, 1997) p.434 opines that 'As with the First World War conscription was not applied to any part of Ireland, though the matter was considered on a number of occasions … the Cabinet in London concluded that "it would be more trouble than it was worth to apply conscription to Northern Ireland".' The decision also had to bear in mind the IRA campaign, mostly in England, that had begun in 1939.

upon the Indian people to give England their support. We felt ashamed for our countrymen, Eire, the only ones to hold back. There is something rather despicable in the Celtic nature mixed with much that is charming and good. They nurse their wrongs. They never forget old grudges. Surely if the Boers and Arabs could forget their grievances, the Irish might. It was absurd to call themselves neutral and shelter behind the British flag and eat food which reached them under the protection of the British navy.

Meantime the Germans were smashing their way towards Warsaw which, shelled and bombarded by land and air, refused to yield. It became a nightmare to hear of the sufferings of these people and it was really a relief when we heard it had yielded. It probably would not have had to do so soon had it not been for the sudden advances of the Russians into Poland.[43] We learnt of this one morning and I must admit we felt a feeling of horror and despondency but later we saw that though poor Poland had this added mincing to suffer, it was really more of a hindrance than a help to Germany though she had tried to make the best of it. Poor Poland was now politically divided. Her government had fled to France and many of her soldiers had crossed to neutral countries.

Very little news was given from France but the French had occupied German lands near Saarbrucken but outside the Siegfried Line.[44] Rumours of discontent in Germany and riots in Czecho-Slovakia came through neutral countries. The Germans continued lying propaganda, saying the British had supplied the Poles with poison gas, giving names of British ships which were still intact but which they boasted they had sunk. They had told so many lies that I doubt if anyone paid much attention to their statements. Then came the news of the sinking of the aircraft carrier *Courageous* by a German torpedoe boat.[45] It was dreadful to think of all the lives lost and one thrilled with admiration for her gallant captain who was last seen saluting the White Ensign.

Generally after the news on the wireless we had a talk from some prominent person, some good, some bad, but Winston Churchill

---

[43] Russia invaded Poland only 16 days after the German attack, on 17 September 1939.

[44] The Siegfried Line was a German defensive wall along its western borders built during the 1930s as part of its re-armament.

[45] HMS *Courageous* was an aircraft carrier sunk in the early months of the war, going down with over 500 crew.

In the Fading Light of a September Day H.M.S. 'Courageous' Lurches to Her Death Plunge

The aircraft carrier
HMS *Courageous* was sunk
with the loss of over
500 lives

outstandingly good. Frank but re-assuring, admitting losses but pointing out gains, talking of the sinking of enemy submarines and the capture of more tonnage than we had lost. This was cheering though we felt it was dreadful to be cheered by the news of sending the crews of submarines to a horrible death, but such is war! I thought of Macbeth 'I have supped full with horrors'.[46] We read of Polish heroes herded together and shot by the Russians; eye-witness accounts of German airmen machine-gunning women and children flying across the fields to seek sanctuary and civilians queuing up for food. 'What man has done to man'! Bismarck is reported to have said he sent millions to their death and plunged millions in grief but he had fixed it with his maker.[47] If true, it seemed a peculiarly German attitude of mind. Man is made in the image of God, we are told, but he had made his God in the image of man.

Sometimes we turned the wireless to Berlin or Hamburg and heard for ourselves the Nazi chiefs: Hitler, hoarse, choked with indignation or

[46] 'I have supped full with horrors. Direness, familiar to my slaughterous thoughts, cannot once start me'. *Macbeth* Act 5 Scene 5.

[47] Otto von Bismarck (1815–98) was responsible for the unification of the German states in the last half of the nineteenth century, principally by engaging in a series of wars with European neighbours.

heard him shouting, yelling his creed.[48] One could feel here was the vision of a madman. Goebbels too, shrieking, howling, cursing. Then back to London and the quiet, controlled, educated voice of an English announcer, if anything too unemotional, telling of our losses at sea, of the French gains in the western front, of our airmen's flights with more propaganda sheets over Germany.

This was a strange war, this one, that started so slowly. When, we asked ourselves, was our army going to take part? What did the Poles, bleeding almost to death, think of our paper war. I can imagine them asking themselves fiercely why, if we could fly unmolested over Germany, did we not drop bombs instead of paper? Hitler seemed encouraged by our methods, as possibly he was intended to be. He made a speech, offering peace terms. Why, he asked now that Poland was conquered, should England wish to plunge Europe into a cruel war? If she did, hers would be the responsibility. Mr Chamberlain replied in a speech re-iterating that there would be no peace signed with the present Nazi government and without guarantees that Germany would withdraw from Poland, Austria and Czecho-Slovakia. A speech from Goebbels followed. He was foaming at the mouth. Then a cry, almost of despair, of the head of the German press, pleading with Roosevelt to intervene. Captured German prisoners told tales of the ignorance of the German people regarding the war. Many did not know they were at war with England and France.

At last we were told that the British army was in France and in the middle of action. We heard a record of the British army. Strangely enough, it was an Irish regiment. We heard the pipes playing *Killaloe*[49] and it was nice to hear the col. saying that there were almost 50–50 men north and south and they got on well. Even if de Valera held back, there were still Irishmen willing to fight beneath the British flag![50] We heard their feet marching, their voices

---

[48] The Duffin family, particularly the seven girls, would have been familiar with the German language. They had been educated at home, prior to attending Cheltenham Ladies' College, by German governesses. Emma had herself spent a year in Germany shortly before the First World War, as a governess.

[49] 'Killaloe', the stirring military march generally associated with Irish regiments in the British army.

[50] Thomas Bartlett and Keith Jeffery, eds., *A Military History of Ireland* (Cambridge University Press, 1997) p. 483 says, 'In 1946 the Dominion Office calculated that over 43,000 men and women "born in Eire" had joined the British services during the war, of whom 32,778 were serving in the army at the end of the war.'

as they sang. Thinking of the men we had nursed and of those who lay buried under countless crosses in France and Belgium, my heart ached to hear them. I remembered lying in my camp bed in France and burying my face in my pillow as I heard the men going up the line to the tunes of 'Will ye no come back again?' and 'The long, long trail'. How many had never come back? Here were their sons starting again on that dreary trail. It seemed incredible, well-nigh insupportable, for those who had lost husbands, fathers, brothers to be asked to give their sons. We were lucky. We had nobody dear or near of age to go in this war.

The news of the sinking of the *Royal Oak* with a loss of 800 men, while at anchor at Scapa Flow, came as a blow.[51] It was so unexpected: no explanation being forthcoming at the time. Then came the news of the first air raid on Oct 17th at the Firth of Forth followed by another that afternoon and the following day. Fifteen men killed on ships but no serious damage done and several aircraft brought down. We wondered if Belfast would come next. We knew its A.R.P. arrangements were said to be far from ready. There were rumours that the Germans had said on the wireless from Hamburg that they would reduce Belfast to a ploughed field for not having remained neutral with Eire but I had not heard it and we had all learnt to discredit rumours of this kind.

Hamburg gives news in English every night but unfortunately at the same time as our own 9 o'clock news. The speaker is sometimes a German speaking excellent English but with a slight accent. At other times a speaker with a perceptible accent who is said by some people most authoritatively to be Baillie Stewart, the British officer who was imprisoned in the Tower for espionage.[52] One evening I believe Countess Zeppelin, who is an English woman with a son by her first marriage at an English public school, spoke saying it was a mistake to think they were short of food; they had plenty of everything.[53] Many who heard her speech spoke of the tragic ring in her voice which suggested that she had been goaded or bullied into making this announcement.

---

[51] The *Royal Oak* was a battleship with many trainees, torpedoed at Scapa Flow and, among the 833 crew who drowned, 120 were boys aged 14–18.

[52] Norman Baillie-Stewart (1909–1966) was a British army officer and active Nazi sympathiser known as *The Officer in the Tower* when he was imprisoned in the Tower of London.

[53] This may be a reference to Mamie McGarvey, daughter of William H. McGarvey, who married Everhard von Zeppelin, Lieutenant in the German Lancers, in 1895.

Explanations of the sinking of the *Royal Oak* were asked for and Winston Churchill paid a tribute to the extraordinary daring and skill of the U-boat commander who, it was thought, must have entered Scapa Flow in the wake of a British vessel and, more strangely still, had escaped again unseen. From the Western front up till past the middle of October we heard little or nothing, The Germans seemed loathe to begin an attack. News of terrific rain in France and abnormal floods in England seemed strange to us who were enjoying dry, beautiful, sunny weather.

I was fairly busy at the Council of Social Welfare.[54] We had been approached by the Ministry of Home Affairs to ask how we would suggest that clothing could be supplied to necessitous children in the event of them having to be evacuated. We consulted with the heads of the chief city missions, the St Vincent de Paul, Salvation Army etc and came to the conclusion that the problem was too big to be tackled by charitable committees. An inquiry from Glasgow, who reported that they had spent £10,000 on clothes confirmed us and we reported to that effect, offering our services to organize but refusing to undertake to supply clothes and boots. Up till Oct 23rd nothing further has been heard from the ministry. Meantime, as we had allowed the G.G. and A.F.A the use of our front room where we carried on our clothing Guild meetings, Olive and I took bales of material home to cut out and I got the Girl Guides and League of Women Helpers to sew them and knit jumpers for us and the Inner Wheel Club (the Women's Rotary) continued to supply and distribute them for us as they had in former winters.[55]

I joined the Alpha Club Hospital Supply meeting which met on Thursdays. We each gave 5/– a month for material and sat sewing many-tailed bandages, helpless shirts etc.[56] I felt as the old soldiers feel at the sight of these. I wanted to be back amongst the Tommies. How many many-tailed bandages had I not put on, how many patients had I not lifted in helpless shirts. Now I was a veteran, too old. I knew I could still be of use dressing wounds and I had my name down for A.R.P 1st aid post but heard nothing.

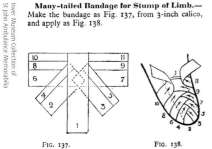

Bryson House, Bedford Street, Belfast became in 1935 the headquarters of the Belfast Council of Social Welfare, of which Emma was Hon. Secretary 1933–53

Many-tailed Bandage for Stump of Limb.— Make the bandage as Fig. 137, from 3-inch calico, and apply as Fig. 138.

FIG. 137.   FIG. 138.

First Aid instructions for many-tailed badges

---

[54] The Belfast Council of Social Welfare had been formed initially in Belfast in 1906 as the Charity Organisation Society. Emma's mother, Maria Duffin, had been one of the founder members. On her demobilisation in 1919 Emma had joined her mother on the committee and served as Honorary Secretary 1933–53. The BCSW archive is in PRONI, D2086.

[55] 'G. G.' may well be the Girl Guides. I have not been able to find what 'A.F.A.' represents.

[56] Officially the 'Gunthorpe (after the inventor) helpless shirt', specifically designed in the First World War for use by wounded soldiers who were immobile and not able to manoeuvre themselves into clothing.

2 VAD Commandant
Stranmillis Military Hospital

Emma's four years' experience (1915–19) serving as a VAD nurse abroad, in Egypt and northern France, and for which service she had been mentioned in dispatches, must have been behind the War Office invitation issued to her early in 1940 to take up the post of Commandant of the VAD unit based at Stranmillis Military Hospital in south Belfast, quite close to the family's Stranmillis home, at *Mount Pleasant*.

As she found out, this turned out to be a wholly different experience from her previous association with the VAD service. It was a largely administrative post which brought her into sometimes frustrating contact with what appeared to her to be somewhat self-defeating, interminable military bureaucracy. This was brought home to her to some degree during the training course at Aldershot, in Hampshire, to which she was sent almost immediately on taking up her post in March ... 'I was not sorry when my fortnight ended'.

One of the, for her, slightly disquieting lessons she learned while at Aldershot was that the changes in the regulations under which VAD nurses served had been relaxed considerably since the First World War. She was, as she put it, 'surprised to learn that there was no special hours for VADs to be in their quarters, also there was no ban upon them entertaining men in their bed-sitting rooms'. And, although she admitted that 'I supposed I must be old-fashioned' she nonetheless 'confessed it would have made me uneasy if I was commandant over, or the parent of, very young girls'. It was with this serious approach to her duties that she returned to Belfast in the spring of 1940 at a time, as she records, when it seemed 'the fate of the British Empire if not ... civilization [was] in the balance'.

May 1940

diary pages 25–49

I wrote this some months ago, Since that I have been called back to the army and the whole situation from my <u>personal</u> point of view has changed. As I feel that the large important events of this war will be recorded elsewhere I intend in this diary to record things from a personal point of view.

As I write this it seems as if the fate of the British Empire, if not the fate of civilization, is in the balance. The Germans have invaded Norway, Denmark, Holland, Belgium, France. One after another they have attacked neutral countries. That most of their successes have been due to diabolical treachery is small comfort. History will relate how they planted spies in every country who made friends, accepted hospitality and betrayed their hosts when the moment arose. The mystery is how these countries, one by one, succumbed, neglected obvious precautions, disregarded warnings, hoped with piteously re-iterated assurances of their neutrality, to stem the German tide of ruthless aggression. Night after night we sat listening to the wireless, another neutral country invaded, more tales of unimagined brutality. Light ships bombed, refugees mercilessly machine-gunned as they trekked wearily from their burning homes. The ships they tried to escape in torpedoed. It is as if the devil himself was in the ascendancy, as if all evil things had risen to overwhelm the good and innocent. History will also relate how the Germans dropped parachutists disguised, armed with explosives, to blow up bridges and important junctions. Wretched boys, shot from aeroplanes to almost certain death. They were as merciless to their own as to their enemies. The lust of power had driven them mad and Europe was in the death grip of a madman. Amidst the horror and confusion the bravery, courage and magnificent heroism of our airmen shines out. Night after night we listen to lists of their marvellous attainments. Forty German aeroplanes a day shot down. One thrills and almost forgets to think of the slaughter. Events follow so quickly. The theatre of war changes so rapidly. To us, 'the man in the street', all is obscure, confused.

Russia invades Finland.[57] We hear only of Finland, listen with horror to accounts from Edward Ward of the Russian soldiers lying dead in thousands. Half fed, half clothed.[58] Frozen. We have hardly realized what

---

[57] The Russian invasion of Finland began on 30 November 1939.

[58] Edward Ward (d.1993) became one of the most enterprising, indeed courageous, foreign correspondents to emerge in the Second World War, reporting from Finland, France and Africa, where he was captured, only being released from the notorious Oflag XIIB in 1945.

this means, are still thrilling to the story of Finland's heroic resistance when Germany invades Norway. Holland is the next victim. The Queen has to fly to England at the risk of her life. Denmark is eaten up, then Belgium's time comes. Belgium, whose wounds from the last war had not healed. Once again we hear of the forts of Namur, of Liege putting up a heroic resistance. Louvain is bombed again. The Germans are once again in Brussels. Less than two years ago we had stood to admire the new library at Louvain, given to the Belgians by the Americans and re-stocked with books from the libraries of the world. Again the Hun had destroyed it. We had read at Brussels the proclamation of Burgomaster Max and I had felt my eyes prick and a lump rise in my throat as I read it, standing with Harry, Celia and Olive in the town hall, on the way back from a motor tour through Germany which had looked peaceful and friendly enough then.[59] What turns this great people into ravening wolves? What madness seizes them, to destroy, to deface, to make the lives of others, of their own, unbearable with horror. Burgomaster Max was alive when we read that proclamation. Now, perhaps happily for himself, he is dead. Who will guide the people of Brussels though this second trial?

News comes though slowly. Everything is secretive, guarded. We have heard so much of the Maginot Line.[60] France was safely entrenched behind it. There was nothing to fear but within a month or two of war the Germans are in Boulogne. History again will relate how this has come to pass. To us it is obscure. Was it treachery or folly that allowed this to happen? Millions has been spent to make the Maginot Line impregnable. To what effect? Its failure has cost us dear. We are told nothing but anyone can realize what the seizure of Boulogne must mean to us in the loss of munitions, food supplies, hospital equipment. They are very near us now. Any night we may hear of England being bombed. The country is looking lovely. The trees are covered with blossom. It is impossible to realize what is going on elsewhere and threatening us.

Since I wrote this the Belgian army has capitulated.[61] We felt almost stunned at this news. The king, whom we had looked on as an heroic figure ready to defend his country to the end, has made terms with

[59] Burgomaster Adolf Max had won fame in August 1914 when, as mayor of Brussels, he had stood in the way of the German invading forces. He died in 1939.

[60] The Maginot Line was a series of fortifications designed to protect France from an invasion by Germany similar to that which had occurred in 1914.

[61] Belgium was invaded by German forces in May 1940.

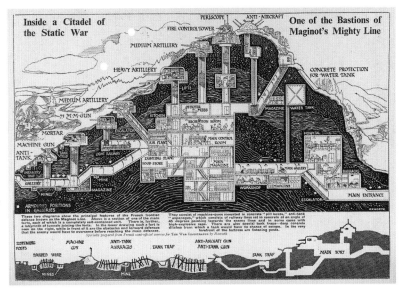

An illustration in *The War Illustrated,* showing the 'impregnable' Maginot Line

Germany without even the courtesy of letting the Allies who had come to his country's aid know what he intended to do. History will judge him. The word 'traitor' rises to everyone's lips. His own government have disowned him but the damage is done. His army has laid down its arms. The French and British have been denied this much-needed aid.

I had not intended to write even so much about public events which can be described by people much better able than I to do so and when they can be seen in their true perspective, but one's own small doings sink into insignificance in the face of such colossal and tragic happenings.

Chamberlain had resigned before this last crisis and Winston Churchill has succeeded him and one cannot but feel he is a better leader though whatever one thinks of Chamberlain's policy one must feel for him, forced to lay down the leadership unwillingly.[62] I always have felt he was too provincial, not sufficiently wide-minded, not a good judge of men, an uninspiring leader, though his integrity and honesty of purpose and sincere desire for peace were qualities to be admired. But Winston Churchill's voice on the wireless inspired confidence and one felt that men could follow such a leader. The King has spoken a simple but inspiring speech, sounding so trusty, so genuine, not a false note and hardly a trace of his usual stammer was apparent. Duff Cooper, the most

---

[62] Neville Chamberlain had resigned as Prime Minister 10 May 1940.

eloquent of all the speakers on the wireless, quiet, restrained, reasoning, warning us of the danger but full of confidence in ultimate victory.[63]

The B.B.C. itself is disappointing, slight, frivolous, programmes uninspired, giving one a feeling that they are fiddling while Rome burns. I switch it off and cannot listen. I try foreign stations. The French, inspired, swift, eloquent, excited but restrained. Germany, like the roar of beasts, come the voices of Hitler, Goering, raucous, thick, coarse voices, hurling invective, threats, curses at the allies. How restrained and dignified our statesmen sound after them.

I had been approached in February to know if I would take the post of Commandant at Stranmillis Mil[iltary] Hospital. I was doubtful, wanted to know what the job was and finally, rather reluctantly, agreed to take it as I had put my name down at the beginning of the war to serve if called on. I wondered if I was doing the right thing in abandoning the B.C.S.W. (Council of Social Welfare) of which I was the Hon. Sec. but after consideration decided I should.[64]

PRONI D2109/20/5

```
No. 2 POSTINGS.

V.A.D. COMMANDANT, Miss Duffin reported for duty at Military
Hospital, Stranmillis, w.e.f. 5. 3. 40.
```

Notification of the posting of 'Miss Duffin' as VAD Commandant, Stranmillis Military Hospital, March 1940

On March 9th I was appointed and made my way up to the hospital.[65] As I passed through the gates I wondered how long I would be there, what sort of work I would be called on to do and inevitably thought of my first day's duty, or rather 'night duty' in hospital at Alexandria, standing bewildered and rather forlorn waiting for the 'night super' to assign me to a ward. I had seen much more life since then. I had more confidence in my own capabilities and was readier to tackle difficulties but, against that, I was older, more disillusioned, less ready to think every new thing interesting, exciting. Life held more possibilities for me in 1915 than it did in 1940. Well, I would have to do my best, and hope I would soon get home again.

[63] Alfred Duff Cooper (1890–1954) was a Conservative MP noted for, among much else, his oratory powers, particularly evident in the parliamentary debate that led to Chamberlain's resignation.

[64] In the event, Emma continued to serve as Hon. Sec. of the BCSW through the war, only resigning her position in 1953.

[65] PRONI D2109/20/5, 'Part 1 Order. No. 58 6.3.40, No. 2 Postings' records that 'VAD Commandant Miss Duffin reported for duty at Military Hospital, Stranmillis w.e.f. 5.3.40 [not 9th as Emma says] (Sgd) D. McVicker Lt-Colonel Commanding Military Hospital, Stranmillis, Belfast.'

Stranmillis Military Hospital nursing staff, including Emma Duffin, bottom right, which the censored newspaper could only report as being 'at a hospital in Northern Ireland'

An aerial photograph of Stranmillis University College Belfast

I first reported to the O.C., Col. McVicker. I had met him before. He was a retired R.A.M.C. and had a private practice in Belfast. He was known both in the army and in civil life as 'Dangerous Dan'. I did not care for him but had heard that he had been pleased at my appointment which was at any rate encouraging. He greeted me in a friendly fashion and took me up to see the quarters for the V.A.D.s and to introduce me to the Matron. I had known the quarters before as I had been there to see the Matron when the Hospital was a college and the students had lived in the quarters.[66]

The college had lent itself in a wonderful way to adaptation as a hospital. It faced the road only a step down from the tramway but it stood in what had been the gardens of a private house. The house stood on a hill and was reserved for an Officers' hospital. Between it and the college were two long white bungalows connected by a central one. In there were the

---

[66] Stranmillis (Teacher) Training College, where the military hospital was located, had been re-located to Fawcett's Hotel in Portrush, Co. Antrim.

PRONI DZ109/20/5

Army Form E664A.

NOTICE PAPER

Voluntary Aid Detachment member enrolled for
employment under the Army Council.

CONDITIONS OF SERVICE

The General Conditions of your enrolment are :—

(a) To serve as a V.A.D. member with the Army for the
period of the present emergency provided that your
services are so long required.

(b) (i) **Mobile Members.**
To perform full-time service at any locality at home
or overseas as may be required.

(ii) **Immobile Members.**
To perform full-time service at a station which may
be rendered from your home without expense to
Army funds for travelling between your home and
place of duty.

(c) To obey all orders given by your superiors.

(d) To remain as a V.A.D. member employed under the
Army until duly discharged.

The normal grounds for discharge are :—

(i) In order to undergo training as a State Registered
Nurse.

(ii) Compassionate grounds.

(iii) Medical grounds.

(iv) For the purpose of being appointed to a commission
in another service.

(v) For the purpose of enrolment into the A.T.S.

(vi) Services no longer required.

Extract from Army Form E664A outlining
the conditions under which members of the
Voluntary Aid Detachment were to serve

sisters' and the V.A.D.s' quarters. I was introduced to a 'Sister Miles', who was acting as House Sister and from whom I hoped to gather information in connection with the messing, but I was soon disillusioned on this point. Sister Miles was squarely built, an English, north country woman, with a strong accent and no H's. Winifred Coey, a friend of my own, was busy cooking and two other V.A.D.s were dusting and sweeping, being hustled and ordered about by Sister Miles.

Miss Quill, the Matron, belonged to the regular army. She was a pretty, attractive woman from Co. Kerry, but seemed worried and distracted. I explained that I had been told I was to go to Aldershot on a fortnight's course under a commandant and was only waiting to know which day, so in the meantime she advised me to get what information I could out of Sister Miles. For the next three days I reported to the hospital but found it difficult to grasp what exactly what my job was to be. 'The V.A.D.s are allowed servants now', said the colonel, producing a rather obscurely worded letter from the W.O.: 'Go to a Registry office and engage two cooks'. I acquiesced but resolved inwardly that it would be quite useless to engage maids till I returned from Aldershot, even if I could get them, and I had reason later to congratulate myself on this decision.

Meanwhile, beyond drinking morning tea with the staff at the quarters I did not seem to make any headway. Sister Miles was either incapable of imparting or unwilling to part with any information. She opened various small rooms importantly and said 'You can keep your butter 'ere' and shut it before I could look round; or, 'I'd an extra store of pillows 'ere. Don't you let the quartermaster know or 'e'll pinch them'. 'Your stores are kept in 'ere'. 'But where do the stores come from, do I order them?', I asked. 'No, they just come', she replied, without any explanation. ''Ere you 'ave to make the list for the N.A.A.F.I. stores but on Monday you make the list. You'll 'ave to do that and arrange the off-duty time. These maids always wanting off duty' etc etc grumble grumble. I had met her kind before, narrow, acquisitive, suspicious and rather greedy. Winifred Coey gave me any information she could. I was allowed by Sister Miles to glance for a second into what was destined to be my sitting room with bedroom and bathroom attached. It looked pleasant enough but she locked the door again firmly.

On March 9th my orders came through to proceed to Aldershot. I had had a busy time trying to get my uniform which was actually only delivered to me hours before it was time for me to start for the train which was agitating, as I had an army pass and had to travel in uniform. Fortunately for me, Marjorie was crossing too, so I had her companionship. We had a good crossing and there were no air raid nor torpedoe boat alarms. The embark[ation] officer greeted me at Larne and saw me safely aboard. Those of us travelling on military passes lined up at a different part of the boat. Once more I realized I was in the army! How it took me back! There was nothing very noticeably different in London, except for the sandbags round the shops and the barrage balloons, like ominous great insects floating in the sky.

As we had crossed on a Saturday and I had had to borrow a uniform hat to travel in and couldn't get one till Monday, I was staying the night in town and Marjorie put me up at her club. On Sunday, as she was meeting a friend, I arranged to go down to see the Crum Ewings at Sevenoaks. In the morning I took a stroll in the park. It was a fine sunny day and the park was full of people in every conceivable uniform. A.T.S.s in khaki, like the W.A.A.C.s of the last war, Wrens, W.R.A.F.s, Red X and St John V.A.D.s and army nurses mingled with the soldiers' uniforms. Most of the latter were in the new 'battledress' which could certainly not be described as smart. It was a one-piece garment which they referred to playfully as their 'Romper suits'.

I found Maud and Nellie Crum Ewing sitting over the dining-room fire. They explained they had not yet 'blacked out' their drawing room which seemed to me a foolish economy as they had their nephew Humphrey and his wife and two children billeted with them, and they all appeared

St John Ambulance service hat

for tea. Maud looked tired, She had served as a V.A.D. in the last war, too, and was now serving at an A.R.P. shelter several days a week and some nights. It was nice to see them again, especially as we felt it might be long before we could meet again.

The next day I went to Scott's to buy a St John hat, even more uncompromising and unbecoming black felt than the ones I had purchased from them in the last war. I then proceeded to report at the headquarters of the St John and Red X at Belgrave Square. I was told that Miss St John Atkinson (query – was she appointed because of her name?) the head of St John was not coming in but I was conducted

Inver Museum Collection of St John Ambulance Memorabilia

upstairs by a gentle little person with a deprecating manner and introduced me to somebody whose name I did not catch. After some desultory conversation with her I was told Dame Beryl Oliver (the head of the Red X) would like to speak to me but as I was leaving the room an imposing female with a 3-cornered hat, much more becoming than we poor junior officers were allowed, stalked in.[67] She asked me questions in a brisk, rather alarming manner. And wrote out chits for my badges and buttons. Later I learnt she was the great Mrs St John Atkinson herself and Gwen Wallace (Asst Controller) in Belfast told me I should have bowed to her and addressed her as 'Madam'. I'm afraid I did neither but she seemed to bear me no ill will as apparently she told Gwen later I was just the type of commandant they wanted.

I was then conducted upstairs where I found Dame Beryl Oliver whom I had remembered reporting to on various occasions at Devonshire House in the last war. She gave me a most friendly greeting and said she remembered seeing us off to Egypt in 1915. I said I thought it was a terrible pity they had made the V.A.D.s privates in this war and she heartily agreed and said they were trying to get it changed. I felt inclined to say 'but why ever did you let them do it, they'll never change them now' but refrained. I lunched at Marjorie's club with her friend Olive Mackey, a very smart, elegant person who was working at the Women's Voluntary Service Bureau. In the afternoon I proceeded to Aldershot and my war work began officially.

Aldershot station swarmed with troops. I took a taxi and proceeded up a very steep hill, past the Cambridge Hospital to a small, shabby, wooden house, Gun Hill House, the sisters' quarters. The House sister greeted me and took me over to the hospital to meet the commandant. The latter, Miss Comac, was a brisk, businesslike, cheerful person who gave me a cheery greeting. She had short cropped uncompromising hair under her Red X uniform hat which was, if anything, a degree more trying than the St John one as it turned up off the face all round. She explained that she had not had quarters for me in the house where she and the Assistant Commandant were billeted so was obliged to put me in amongst the

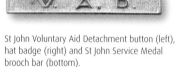

St John Voluntary Aid Detachment button (left), hat badge (right) and St John Service Medal brooch bar (bottom).

Inver Museum Collection of St John Ambulance Memorabilia

---

[67] Dame Beryl Oliver (1882–1972) had been commanding officer of the Voluntary Aid Detachment organisation in the First World War and continued to serve on associated committees during the Second World War.

V.A.D. rank and file. I made no objection and she took me and my luggage in her car back past the hospital to a square surrounded by married quarters.

The V.A.D.s were billeted in the married quarters, six or eight people in each house, two generally in a flat which consisted of two rooms, a bed-sitting room and a bedroom off it. My stable companion was a nice girl called Thatcher, a V.A.D. clerk. She was already established in the bed sitting room so I was given the back bedroom. The clerks did not breakfast till 8.30 as they did not go on duty till 9 but Comac said she breakfasted with the sisters at 8 so of course I had to do the same. The billet was quite 10 minutes walk or more from the hospital. My first purchase was an alarm clock. I realized I was a good deal older since the last war and felt discomforts more acutely as I had to stand on my dressing table to roll up an improvised black blind. Rise by an alarm clock at 7.15 and wait till a kettle boiled before I could get some warm water to wash as, though there was a bathroom, there was no hot water.

The bed was narrow and as hard as a brick, only brown blankets and not enough, very coarse sheets too narrow for the bed and dingy in colour, no pillow, only a small, round, hard object called a bolster but it might as well have been a billet of wood and would have suited a Chinese lady better than me. Thatcher was kind and hospitable, lent me a feather pillow for which I was profoundly grateful and gave me a cupful of Ovaltine going to bed. I put my heavy overcoat on the bed but it constantly slipped off and I cannot say I slept peacefully. However, it was war work! It was bitterly cold in the early morning walk to the sisters' quarters. The food there was very bad and the breakfast not too ample due, I later discovered, more to bad housekeeping than shortness of rations.

The little dining room was far too small to accommodate all the sisters. There were a great many from New Zealand who had joined up. Jolly girls with colonial accents, ready for anything. There were several regulars in their red capes. Some of them seemed mere children to me especially two, an Irish and Scottish girl. The former was most attractive, with lovely eyes and the proverbially good Irish complexion. She was invariably late for breakfast and joined the other late-comers, who had to sit as if in disgrace at the side table, faces to the wall, as there was not sufficient accommodation at the centre table. 'Oh girls', she appealed, her brogue getting stronger and stronger, 'for pity's sake, is there no breakfast for me again, not as much as a bit of toast?'. After breakfast I went with Comac, the commandant, to Cambridge House, a house standing alone which had been destined for a V.A.D. mess and recreation rooms but had, Comac told me, always so far been used to accommodate V.A.D.s who were sick, not sick enough to be in hospital but too sick to be left in quarters. Comac and the Assistant Commandant, Crompton-Roberts slept there, also an unpaid V.A.D. who looked after the sick. I read the paper and waited for Comac who presently appeared and took me over to the hospital, a large yellow-brick building with miles of corridors.

She took me to a bleak, drafty office which she and Crompton-Roberts shared with the Sergt. Major and an N.C.O and private about 3ft in height who seemed to concentrate continually on lines of figures which they checked. The commandants' whole office consisted of a table which seemed in rather a state of disorder. It was set between the corridor and the door which was constantly open so that one sat in a perpetual draught and before long I developed a bad cold. Comac took me along to introduce me to the Matron, Miss Davis, a 'buy out'.[68] She looked to me tired and weary but had a dry sense of humour that appealed to me. The Assistant Matron was a Miss Ivers who shortly before had been on a boat that was torpedoed on its way back from India. She looked frail and wistful and I imagine was suffering from shock. She had lost all her belongings.

For the next day or two I followed round at Comac's heels picking up all the information I could about the work of commandants. Comac was a seriously-minded person who was very pleasant to work with but was rather lacking in a sense of humour. She must I think have been one of the first commandants in a military hospital. She had been on a trip to Kenya and at the time of the Munich crisis had flown home to join her Red X unit and offer her services. She had joined up with her detachment and they had had a hard deal. On the usual English system of muddling through they had been called up and sent to Aldershot without any preparations to receive them. They had been given a list of householders on whom they could be billeted and had trekked the whole way from house to house rejecting or being rejected. Somehow or other they had eventually found sleeping quarters. It was then found that there was nobody to deal with the many questions arising and Comac, being of the

---

[68] A 'buy out' refers to a regular soldier who has paid a sum of money to terminate their service.

type suitable for authority, had been selected by the Matron as a sort of official commandant. Eventually, the V.A.D. council had realized that a permanent commandant was really essential, had interviewed and appointed her and later Crompton-Roberts to assist her. The latter was a very different type, much more easy-going and unofficial with a much greater sense of comfort.

It was interesting to compare the modern V.A.D.s with the 1914–19 ones. They were, as was to be expected of this generation, much more independent than we had been. They got their off-duty time there regularly; had three nights off after night duty (only a month's) where we had had one after two months. Their day off was a reality not a possibility once a month and was given in addition to their ½ day of the week so that, if they lived near, they could get home for the night. I was surprised to find how many of them had cars of their own and there was hardly a house in the married quarters that had not a car parked outside the door. They seemed a nice lot of girls on the whole, and considering most of them came from luxurious homes there seemed little grumbling. It seemed to me hard that there was no communal sitting room, only a dining hall at the hospital and if they spent their off-duty time in their own quarters they had to light their own fires which meant not only cleaning the stoves but breaking up large lumps of coal and chopping up packing cases which were used as a ration.

There were over 100 V.A.D.s and as each one got a day off once a month one of the chief jobs of the commandant was filling in passes for them These passes seemed to me ridiculously elaborate. First they were filled in by the commandant with the V.A.D.'s name, army number, the day she was to be allowed absent from quarters etc. This had then to be taken to the sister of the ward for signature, then to hospital office to get the stamp on it and the Co. officer's signature for the C.O. and Matron's signature. All through the morning the V.A.D.s dropped in asking for passes and I filled in a good many for Comac as the day after I arrived Crompton-Roberts went on leave. After that we chased round to get the other signatures, wasting a lot of time as, as often as not, Matron was not in her room when we went or if she was then the company officer was not in his office, and this involved hanging about, or pursuing him round the hospital. Comac also dealt with complaints from irate mothers who thought their daughters were not being properly looked after when ill, investigated complaints about petty thefts in the quarters, saw the medical

44

A Second World War steel helmet
with the St John Ambulance insignia

Inver Museum Collection of St John Ambulance
Memorabilia

officer about patients already sick, or who had reported sick, signed in new girls on a form known as E6.33, made lists for inoculation, vaccinations etc., saw that new girls were issued with 'tin hats' and fitted with gas masks etc etc.

She took her job very seriously but I couldn't quite see, except when they had many sick (which they had had, for the place was stirring with German measles) what she and Crompton-Roberts were so busy about. She was most regimental: stood at attention when addressing an M.O. and interpolated 'sir' after every sentence. The company officer, a rather young and shy M.O., looked to me rather embarrassed by this, though of course she was officially correct. Still, I thought it a bit heavy-handed and Matron used to say 'oh, for goodness sake, sit down, why are you both standing?'. The col. was a peppery little fellow of the old school who was I think the only one who probably approved of the regimental attitude.

When I got to know her better I told her I thought the sheets and bolsters in the V.A.D.s' beds were disgraceful. She looked slightly worried but said 'As a matter of fact I rather like the bolsters'. I felt after that that, though she would be most conscientious, the V.A.D.s would not receive much consideration in the comfort line from her. Thatcher, who had a sense of comfort, said rather plaintifully [sic plaintively] and, I felt, with justice, 'I do feel Comac might do a little more for us but I suppose it's difficult for her, having been an ordinary V.A.D. and she herself doesn't mind discomfort. She went across Africa alone in a Baby Austin or something like that.[69] Comac never took any off duty time when Crompton-Roberts was on leave though for the life of me I couldn't see any reason why she shouldn't. I was determined I was not going to walk step by step with her in that way and to do her justice I don't think she expected me to.

I began getting in touch with various people fairly near whom I wanted to see, especially as I thought I would probably not be in England for a long time again. I spent an afternoon with Dora Bald who took me to see Tom and Iris Sinclair, who lived nearby. Another day I met Germaine Eggar at

---

[69] The Austin 7 car, nicknamed 'the baby Austin' was one of the most popular cars produced in pre-war Britain. Its social impact has been compared with that of the Model T Ford in the United States.

Guildford. She had come half-way from Epsom to meet me. It was horrid cold day and we sat in the coffee room of a gloomy hotel and discussed the war and all our mutual friends and relations. Her John had been rejected for service, much to her relief, because of a bad mastoid operation. Iris and Tom, on the other hand, had had their two boys, Christopher and Michael, in the army and the 3rd, John, waiting to be called up. Poor Iris was already in a nervous state and I felt sorry for Tom. One day I went to town and met *Dorfy* and Dawn.[70] I lunched with them at the V.A.D.s' club and wondered, as I parted from them in the underground, how long it would be before I would see them again, and how old Dawn would be.

My fortnight at Aldershot seemed a long one to me and I was glad I hadn't to face the prospect of a long period there. The weather continued bitterly cold with a biting wind and heavy showers. There were hundreds of Canadian troops who had not been long there and were still carrying only civilian gas masks. Once a week everyone in the Cambridge hospital had to work for ½ an hour in their gas masks, a wise precaution. One day there was a parade to see that all gas masks were in good order and

A lady's gas mask in case
NIWM Collection

Comac left me in charge of her desk to deal with anything that cropped up. The first thing was a girl reporting sick. She confessed she had been in a motor accident the day before but had not reported it. On cross-examination as she could not even remember whether the car had turned

---

[70] There were four members of the wider Duffin family named Dorothy, including Emma's sister-in-law *Dorfy*.

over or not, I decided that she was either suffering from shock or concussion and refused to let her go back to her quarters. I took her over to Cambridge House, told the V.A.D. in charge to put her to bed and to report to the M.O. who attended to V.A.D.s and sick sisters. He was a strange individual who for some reason always wore civilian clothes, a scholarly looking man who stood about imparting information to us on medical subjects and issuing diatribes against war. He always referred to German measles as Rubella and ordinary measles as Morbilla, which amused us as I had served for 9 months in an Isolation hospital in the last war and never heard these scientific terms.

Another girl dropped in to report that her stable companion was sick and unable to go on duty. She described their billets and I set forth to visit the invalid. It was quite 15 minutes' walk from the hospital in another barrack square. I couldn't get any reply at the front door so I wandered round to the back, got in and visited every room in the house but found no sign of the patient. I returned disconsolately and found a list on Comac's table of the V.A.D.s and where they were on duty. I found she was working in the Co. cookhouse so after ascertaining where it was, I pursued her there and ran her to earth. She said she had felt better so just came on duty. I was glad I had not taken the M.O. on a wild goose chase. One of the sisters appeared later to say her V.A.D. was being very sick so I visited her, took her back to her quarters and procured glucoseate from Cambridge House for her. I think Comac was quite glad I was there to help while Crompton-Roberts was on leave.

I was surprised to learn that there was no special hours for V.A.D.s to be in their quarters, also there was no ban upon them entertaining men in their bed-sitting rooms. Comac seemed to see no cause for disquietude on this score and I supposed I must be old-fashioned but confessed it would have made me uneasy if I was commandant over, or the parent of, very young girls. One of the V.A.D.s, a married woman with a son at Eton, did tell Comac she thought she ought to know that two of the V.A.D.s whom she thought were really quite nice, entertained men till after midnight. Comac admitted she thought this undesirable but pointed out that it was difficult as they were scattered in so many different quarters for her to keep an eye on them all.

3 CALM BEFORE THE STORM

On her return to Belfast Emma was confronted at uncomfortably close quarters by the inflexible army administrative machine as she sought to make conditions for the nurses in her charge as acceptable as possible. She quickly concluded, on finding that 'Every possible difficulty was put in the way', that 'the fighting in France [that she herself had experienced] was nothing to the fighting that went on to get anything done in the army'. Nonetheless her administrative capacity was up to the challenge, when she confided to Matron that she had not enough to do she was told it was because they each were 'good organisers'.

Her comments on the extent to which rationing was impacting on living standards in Northern Ireland are enlightening. 'After a year and a half of war', she confides, 'the food in Ulster is ample'. Later in the year, she facilitates the VADs and other hospital staff in organising as sumptuous a Christmas dinner as the rationing regulations allowed. 'If Hitler could have seen that dinner it would have depressed him', she concludes, before listing the range of food on the menu.

She was allowed to live at home at the beginning of her Belfast posting, during which time she confirms that extent to which her family, and no doubt countless other families throughout Northern Ireland and Great Britain, depended on the radio for information as the war progressed. Nonetheless, Emma maintains her earlier disappointment with the level of information produced by the BBC admitting that its difficulties 'must have been enormous... but the results for the ordinary listeners were certainly disappointing.' Her response to watching a film recounting some of the early atrocities evident in German concentration camps (she left early) betokens the extent to which the barbarism of the Second World War, at home and in Europe, would magnify in the immediate future.

diary pages 50–86

I was not sorry when my fortnight ended and I returned after an uneventful journey home to take up my duties at Stranmillis. My first job was to get my own and the V.A.D.s' quarters ready as at present they were sleeping in the top bungalow which was on higher ground but joined to the lower one by two common rooms and the dining room. I found Miss Quill, the Matron, had been very ill with pneumonia since I left and there was only a sister in charge. I continued for some time to live at home and came in daily and set about engaging maids.[71] I had been given a copy of a W.O. letter authorising two cooks and two maids for 30 V.A.D.s. I noticed with dismay that, until the numbers of V.A.D.s increased to 70, the same staff had to do. I wondered if I got 75 what would happen. However, sufficient for the day. At present I had only 32. I thought I had only to proceed to engage the maids but I was soon disillusioned. The W.O. letter was not sufficient authority. A letter of authorisation was required from the A.D.M.S. but the letter must go through the Matron and the C.O. Accordingly I drafted a letter, quoting the number, date etc of the W.O. letter and asking for permission to engage the maids. I had been told by Comac that she had been taught that an official letter to the C.O. or Matron must begin 'Madam' or 'Sir' and ending 'I am, Your obedient servant'. Accordingly, I followed instructions and typed a letter on these lines, which was duly approved by the Matron and C.O. but I was told not to engage the maids till the authority from the A.D.M.S. came through. This took some days and meantime Sister Miles continued to 'boss' at her own sweet will at the quarters and regarded us if not with animosity at any rate with disapproval. Eventually I engaged two house maids and got down to getting the quarters in the lower bungalow ready for the migration of the V.A.D.s that were still housed in the upper bungalow. The maids muttered sulkily that there was plenty of work to be done and I foresaw that there would be domestic troubles.

I was entitled to two cooks, one with wages from 15/– to £1 weekly but I knew two cooks would quarrel and as no scullery maid or kitchen maid was allowed for I knew they would never agree who was to do the scrubbing and cleaning. I decided to engage a lady cook at £1 weekly and a kitchen maid who could be called a cook on the official papers at 12/6 a week. I was lucky in securing a Miss Teasdel who had worked under the cook at the Riddel Hall and was strongly

---

[71] The Duffin family house at Mount Pleasant, Stranmillis Road was less than half a mile from Stranmillis Military Hospital.

recommended.[72] I engaged two kitchen maids who never turned up but by dint of pressing V.A.D.s and convalescent patients I managed. Meantime, a letter arrived from the A.D.M.S. asking why I had engaged the 2nd cook at a lower wage than the other as it appeared to be the W.O. policy to allow for good cooks and that the food should be properly served and cooked. I wrote a polite but rather tart letter back, saying the W.O. had not permitted a kitchen or scullery maid and I could assure them that I thought the arrangement that I had made would prove satisfactory (which it did) and I had no further letter. The irony of the situation was that Matron was only allowed to pay her cook £35 and as she could not get a satisfactory one at these wages she was bombarding the A.D.M.S. with letters to obtain permission to pay higher wages while my two had meanwhile to cook for both messes. I have recorded this in detail because it was my first initiation into the 'army' way of conducting affairs and what I called 'men's housekeeping'. Every possible difficulty was put in the way. I said bitterly later that the fighting in France was nothing to the fighting that went on to get anything done in the army.

Meanwhile I was learning the ropes, getting acquainted with all the A.F.s and A.C.I.s (Army Forms, Army Council Instructions) learning to find my way round the hospital and which of the N.C.O.s, staff sergeants, quartermaster sergeants, sergeant majors etc to apply to. The colonel was easy to get on with when one had sized him up. He may or may not have been a good doctor, but good organizer he was not. He was a great procrastinator and put off putting his signature to many of the forms that were piled before him. He had a pleasant way of telling V.A.D.s that he would make them N.C.O.s or procure higher rates of pay for them regardless of the fact that he could not carry out his promises. As a rule he was easy-going but every now and then he would scowl and throw his weight about but if one stood up to him he generally collapsed into geniality again. I had sized him up from the first and knew that all his statements were far from accurate but I never let him see that I suspected this and actually I got on very well with him. He had a weakness for the aristocracy and had a way of referring to influential people by their Christian names though I knew he had only a slight acquaintance with them. He had a disarming way of telling you frankly that he could not sign papers as he was going to the Maze races and I heard him on the

72 Riddel Hall, where Emma's sister Ruth was principal from 1914 to 1943, had been established in 1913–14 as a hall of residence for female students at Queen's University.

50

telephone asking the A.D.M.S. to postpone a visit as he had a meeting of the polo club on that date.[73] I felt that he was riding for a fall and I was proved right later.

Meanwhile, Miss Quill had been replaced by Miss Miller, who had arrived from England to take over one morning. She was a regular, a red cape, a short, stout, roundabout person, good nature personified, with bright eyes which took in and sized up people and things. I learnt, when I knew her later, to appreciate her greatly. She had a keen sense of humour, was human and sympathetic in all her dealings but knew when to be firm and, if necessary, stern. She had a great sense of comfort and soon decided to end Sister Miles' career in the quarters. She was up in army forms and knew every trick to wrangle or procure funds or necessary authorisations to obtain necessities either for hospital or for the nurses. From the first I felt there is the right person in the right place. She had just come from a C.C.S. (Casualty Clearing Station), near Amiens.

One of her first acts was to put Sister Miles on night duty in the hospital and then, having taken the reins and, as important, the keys into her own hands, she and I proceeded to open store rooms and explore all Sister Miles's 'hidie holes'. We counted and sorted linen, took inventories of china etc, released curtains and bed covers for use, got patients up from hospital to put polish on the floors and brasses. Soon the place looked quite different. I moved down my V.A.D.s to the lower bungalow and moved in to my own quarters. I put flowers in the sitting room and on the dining room tables and hung some pictures, reproductions from old masters, in the sitting room and Paul Henry posters in the dining room.[74] Matron asked me to take over the housekeeping for the sisters' mess, as well as the V.A.D.s' and meanwhile she had secured a lady cook too, so things began to move more smoothly.

An Order of St John branded feeding cup
Inver Museum Collection of St John Ambulance Memorabilia

I found that everything under the colonel was done unofficially, which was rather surprising as he was an ex-R.A.M.C. The hospital took its tone from him. V.A.D.s faded out and I heard unofficially that they were on sick

---

[73] Down Royal racecourse is situated at The Maze, near Lisburn, Co. Antrim.

[74] Paul Henry (1877–1953) a Belfast-born artist noted for his paintings of Connemara landscapes in a spare post-impressionist style.

leave or having nights off. I found it impossible to keep stock of them at all but Matron and I soon altered that. I insisted on being told officially if they were granted leave and instituted passes for those spending nights out of quarters. I had a meeting and spoke to them all and asked them if they wanted anything. I was inundated with questions about their pay. Being privates they had to parade for their pay, which never by any chance was what they were supposed to get.

Mr Bell, the company officer, said he only paid them what came for them from Holywood, the headquarters of 15 Coy, to which we belonged. He seemed rather to resent my asking questions about them, but I was firm and said it was my business. I found if any of the V.A.D.s were busy, or away, or on night duty, another one was just handed her pay. I instituted that no-one was to draw anyone else's pay without a chit of authorization which again Mr Bell seemed puzzled about but I think he saw the point when it turned out that a mistake had been made in the payments and a V.A.D. on night duty said she hadn't had her pay. The matter was cleared up and I think Mr Bell saw my system was right.

The colonel insisted that he and I should visit Col. Lambkin in Holywood to inquire why the pay was different from that laid down in an A.C.I. (Army Council Instruction) which dealt with V.A.D.s and their rates of pay. Mr Bell was distinctly sulky and we departed in an ambulance driven by a very elegant 'Fanny'. I felt annoyed with Mr Bell's attitude as I felt I was only doing my duty in trying to solve the mysteries of the pay system. Poor Mr Bell! After all, he had joined as a doctor, not as an accountant and perhaps it was hardly to be wondered at that he felt annoyed. Later we got to know each other better and made common cause in fighting injustices and ferreting out mistakes. We got very little information from Col. Lambkin who was pleasant but obviously thought V.A.D.s a nuisance and referred all the difficulties to a very young, rather supercilious, staff sergeant. I fought that fight for many a day before the matter was satisfactorily cleared up.

Between our colonel and Col. Lambkin there was no love lost. Our colonel resented being under Holywood and did his best to inflict pin pricks. He was delighted if any flaw in Holywood administration could be found and, rather to my dismay, announced one day that he intended to go to Holywood himself and I was to go too. Matron wanted to go to visit the Matron at Holywood so we all went in his large car driven by his daughter (a Fanny) accompanied by a young naval man to whom she had just got engaged. When we arrived at Holywood they all went in for tea but our colonel and I proceeded to Col. Lambkin's room. Col. Lambkin was outwardly pleasant but he and [the] colonel were like two cats in a roll and I knew nothing would be gained by the expedition. Strangely enough, our colonel, who had been full of what he intended to say and what he meant to point out at Holywood, in Col. Lambkin's presence rather collapsed. He had promised Miss Moore, one of the clerks, that he would make her a sergeant and Col. Lambkin told him he couldn't do it. He had boasted to me that he was going to do it but, when it came to the point, he accepted Col. Lambkin's decision more or less meekly and contented himself by having her made a corporal. I had a struggle with him over the promotion of the cooks. He wanted to make one of the youngest and most unsuitable ones an N.C.O. for no reason but that she was the daughter of a local doctor but I won and insisted they should be ranked according to their capabilities.

As things got more ship-shape I found I had less and less to do and was able to help Matron who was rather overcome to find masses of stores from the Red X, which her predecessor had apparently made no effort to list or arrange. We spent two mornings counting masses of operation stockings, abdominal bandages, pyjamas etc and I made her a card index of all the places they came from. I wrote her out particulars of the staff in her book and fixed up a board showing where they were all working on cards that could be slipped in and out as she wanted to move them, which delighted her heart.

My chief worry was the V.A.D.s' rations. I had now secured my maids, my lady cook and a rather inefficient kitchen maid and had the domestic arrangements running fairly smoothly but I found the solving of the rations question beyond me. Nobody seemed able to find me clear information. Sister Miles' explanation, that they just came, was not altogether true. The meat, bread, sugar and flour 'just came'. That's to say the quartermaster ordered them from the R.A.S.C. according to the numbers in the mess. The dry goods etc we could order from the 'N.A.F.F.I.' i.e. the army stores.[75] This sounds simple but, alas, it was not. The quartermaster, Captain V., was pleasant but unpractical and unbusinesslike. A wine-

---

[75] This is a misprint of 'NAAFI' representing the 'Navy, Army and Air Force Institute' that had been established after the First World War to coordinate and rationalise the provision of services and supplies, including food, to non-commissioned ranks in the armed forces.

taster by profession, he knew nothing of a q.m.'s job and the corporal in the office still less. They ordered the wrong amounts, lost the delivery chits, made muddles. In vain, I tried to fathom the mystery of a terrible form called the A.B.48. It was possibly suited to feeding battalions of men on, and when fully understood by a trained clerk may have been worked successfully but with a staff of amateurs the results were disastrous.

In vain I reported to the col. that it was not being properly kept. He waved his hand airily and said 'Oh, that must be done. Tell Sheila Walsh to do it in her spare time'. Sheila Walsh was a cheery little nursing V.A.D. who, having worked in her father's office and having some head for figures, was picked upon to cope with it. I insisted it should not be in her spare time but she must be put onto it as part of her duties, which was eventually done. But she was defeated by it eventually, chiefly because the office failed to supply her with the necessary statistics. I imagine the A.T.S.s, W.A.A.F.s etc had also found it beyond them and we felt that was why at a later date we were all out on field service rations.

Capt V. (Q.M.) produced a large packet of paper as large as [a] bound volume of Punch and said he thought I had better fill in the daily parade sheet every morning. I innocently accepted it but, on further study, I discovered the packet consisted of loosely printed sheets about 8" by 12" on which was printed the name of every imaginable live man or animal that could in any way be supposed to be connected with the British army. Drummer boys sick and drummer boys well, prisoners in health and sickness, horses and mules in lines or smitten with illness: everything I found only, alas, V.A.D.s had been omitted! Bearing in mind the instructions frequently issued on the wireless and in the press to 'save paper', I returned Capt V. his imposing packet and asked him if he did not think a chit of about 3" by 4" stating how many V.A.D.s were in mess would meet the case and he rather doubtfully admitted that it would.

He was a rotten Q.M. and very unpopular though I think he was well-meaning enough. He showed up at his best at hospital concerts which he organised and enjoyed as much [as] or more than the patients. Sitting at these concerts, listening to the old songs, surrounded by men in blue, sisters in scarlet capes and V.A.D.s in the same uniforms we had worn I felt often we had stepped back into the past. Again and again the feeling of incredulity which many others must have experienced swept over me. If during the last war I had been able to see into the future and see myself in practically the same surroundings over 20 years later I would have shrunk from it in horror. Mercifully we did not foresee then what was to come.

Meanwhile the war proceeded. With startling rapidity event followed event. The capitulation of Belgium was stunning. Then came the news of the evacuation from Dunkirk, well described as an epic in British history. The sudden collapse of France left us gasping. All we had heard of the impregnability of the Maginot Line was recalled. Week after week this had been dinned into us. *The Illustrated London News* had wearied us with drawings of it. What had happened? That such a folly could ever have been committed by responsible people as to leave a badly guarded opening in the line seemed incredible, unforgiveable. That Pétain, old man though he was, the hero of Verdun, could have fallen so low as to sue for an armistice seemed unthinkable.[76] One read of the French entering the railway carriage in which the armistice in the last war had been signed, with shame and resentment. My heart burned for the French. For this shameful betrayal by their politicians. Through it all I never heard from anyone the suggestion that we should fail as the other nations had failed, never a murmur of the word defeat, never a suspicion that the Germans could beat us; nor have I ever heard it since. I feel, and every man, woman and child in the British Islands feels, we shall conquer. Winston Churchill's speeches were a joy to listen to. Warning us of dangers to come, of difficulties to be overcome, of sacrifices to be made, but always encouraging, the voice of a leader of men, expressing his confidence of victory. Duff Cooper and Eden spoke well, too, and I for one never felt a regret that Chamberlain was gone, though I could pity him.

Sisters were posted to us from England, some of whom had been through the evacuation. One little Scotch sister who had lost everything and had been through terrible times in a bombed hospital train and a bombed ship, still was able to smile and looked unbroken. Matron put her in as Home sister and I saw a lot of her and liked her. Her name was McGeary. She was conscientious and all for discipline but combined with it a great

Herself an illustrator, Emma Duffin comments in her diary on wartime cartoonists, some of whose work featured in *The Illustrated London News*

NIWM collection

---

[76] Marshal Philippe Pétain (1856–1951) Prime Minister of France signed the armistice with Germany 22 June 1940 and remained head of what became known as the Vichy government. He was tried for treason after the war.

sense of humour and when she had a touch of lipstick on and cocked her uniform hat at a becoming angle she could look as frivolous as anybody. She did not talk much of her experiences at first but she had been in a railway carriage with machine gun bullets coming through the window. She had walked along the embankment giving morphine to French civilians. She had crawled under a burning railway carriage to rescue a full bottle of brandy for her wounded. She had fed for three days on a tin of pineapple and come up smiling. Another sister, Luxton, arrived. She looked nervy and had a horror-stricken look in her eyes which it took time to eradicate. She had a dark, narrow, rather wooden face but her eyes smouldered and she confessed she could not sleep.

A telephone message informed us a Gen. Hosp. Matron and 23 sisters were to arrive one night. Matron and I and some volunteers sat up to welcome them. They were due at midnight and we had supper laid but midnight came and passed and at 1am Matron telephoned to try and ascertain their whereabouts. She was told it was 'secret' but they were coming. At 2am we went to bed; at 4 they arrived, complete with luggage and camp kit. Miss McGeary and I laboured to feed this increased flock with the help of our good little lady cooks, both under 20.

The V.A.D.s had been taken off the A.B.48 form, probably because nobody could master it, and drew rations instead. Plentiful and good but so badly distributed. Pounds of rice and dried beans, mountains of cheese and bread but no green vegetables except for an occasional sack of unappetizing-looking cabbages and only a small 1/2 tumblerful of milk per head for tea, porridge and cooking. For weeks I struggled to get these rations more sensibly divided but it was like knocking one's head against a stone wall. It enraged me to listen to talks on the wireless about the value of milk and fresh vegetables and fruit and to read in the paper that the troops drew fresh green vegetables 5 days a week. We knew it wasn't true.

Before these extra sisters had arrived I had been sent by the A.D.M.S. up to Derry to report on the welfare of the V.A.D.s there. Harry Randall was going up on a tour of inspection in his capacity of welfare officer, so he got permission to take me in his car.[77] We started on rather a wet morning but even that didn't destroy the beauty of the drive, part of it through Lord

---

[77] Captain Harry Randall was married to Celia, Emma's younger sister.

O'Neill's estate where a blue carpet of bluebells was spread beneath the lovely green of the spring trees. The hospital at Derry was in the barrack square. It was very old and rather gloomy looking and had only really been a reception station before the war. The sisters' mess was in a small house in the corner of the square and the V.A.D.s' mess was on the third side of the square. The fourth side of the square was on Lough Foyle facing Derry.[78] It was very cold and exposed but there was something rather fascinating about it and there was a lovely view up and down the Foyle river. The Matron, or rather sister-in-charge, was a red-cape (regular), Sister Holmes. Poor thing, she had been home on long leave from India and had been posted here. What a contrast.

There were only two other sisters in the mess. They were friendly and made me comfortable and I was taken over to be introduced to the colonel. His name was Otway and he came from Waterford and seemed to nurse a grievance against all the world. He looked at me rather suspiciously and I think wondered what I was there for and I felt a bit of an intruder. The V.A.D. quarters seemed to me very bleak. They were ample enough and could have been made comfortable but the furniture in the sitting room consisted of two broken down chairs, given by people in Derry, 2 deck chairs and a square of linoleum bought, so I was told, by Mrs O'Brien, one of the V.A.D.s. Mrs O'Brien was a rather imposing person, quite unsuited by temperament to be a nurse. She was artistic and Irish!! She had done quite a clever scene, like a theatre curtain on the rather bleak walls of the sitting room. She seemed to be full of rather vague grievances and I gathered she was rather a trial to both V.A.D.s and Matron. She had a daughter, a V.A.D. cook who was, I was told, quite undisciplined and quite disinterested in cooking. She was rather an attractive young thing with a freckly nose and fair hair brushed straight back from her face and wide intelligent blue eyes. I listened to grievances, pointed out things that might be done, and returned to Stranmillis to write a report and recommendations which I doubt were probably never carried out.

Matron gave me a warm welcome and had my room all dressed and fresh flowers in it. Spring had come and the grounds of the hospital were full of daffodils. It was not long after my return that the twenty-three sisters and their Matron arrived and rather disturbed our peace, especially as a

---

[78] Ebrington Barracks, Derry

CCS with another 8 sisters turned up too. They brought no servants so charwomen had to be engaged and Miss McGeary and I had a job organizing and getting everyone fed and housed. The Matron of the hospital was a very seriously-minded individual, very English and totally devoid of humour. She did not pull well with my Matron who took what we call in Ireland a 'scunner' at her.[79] Unfortunately, she shared her sitting room and had a very aggravating way of leaving her papers about or having sisters in to be interviewed, which exasperated Matron. 'What does she think she's doing? She hasn't even a hospital but she never stops writing letters and asking questions', she said indignantly. She certainly did seem to make rather heavy weather of everything. 'Typical St Thomas's', snorted my Matron who, I must confess, judged her very harshly but then you cannot have two queens in one hive! Miss Bridges was her name and she was an old Cheltonian and I who was one too recognized the type – 'conscientious, churchy, hard-working, rather weary'. I was sorry for her as she seemed lonely and I took her out once or twice but she did not attract me.

The col. had been transferred to England and we heard rumours that he had been at Dunkirk. His successor was a very different type: a dry little stick, inclined to fuss, and far too dependent on the sgt. major who held him in the hollow of his hand. He was a nice little man and very straight which was more than could be said about our late col. He had nice manners and was courteous except occasionally when he got into a flap about something and grew snappy and strangely unreasonable. He told me he was very lonely so I took him out to several houses. He did not stay very long and was eventually replaced by Col. Booth, a southern Irishman whom I liked better than either of his predecessors. He was handicapped by being rather deaf but he had the advantage of a sense of humour.

Meanwhile the big air raids in England started.[80] We listened to the news which was meagre and rushed to the papers which told us little but bit by bit we realized what was happening and wondered when our turn would come. I was amazed that no preparation was made at the hospital or quarters. Our quarters had been supplied by the former inmates with fire

---

[79] In the Ulster dialect 'to take a scunner at' someone or something is to dislike it/them heartily.

[80] The Luftwaffe raids on British cities began on London 7 September 1940 and gradually spread to other cities.

58

hose but I made my V.A.D.s have fire practices but it was not till nearly a year later that a shelter was built and stirrup pumps and sand bags for incendiary bombs supplied. The Germans' bombing of open towns and civilian populations was horrible and indefensible but after what they had done in Holland, Poland etc only to be expected. There will be plenty of accounts of those cruel bombings by those who experienced them so I need not do more than record our reactions. In a strange way, after a time one seemed numbed by the repetition of horrors, even found one's attention wandering while the voice on the wireless described the raids. This was not a unique experience. Many people told me they had reacted similarly. Strange that repetition of what was a ghastly experience to individuals should end by becoming monotonous, even boring. One heard unmoved of the slaughter of German pilots and even the tragic announcement 'One of our aircraft failed to return' ceased, except occasionally, to impress one.

I think it is worth recording that I have never yet heard anyone suggest that we could lose this war. Even Italy's entrance into it, even the bombing of London, the destruction of Coventry, did not shake our confidence. Mussolini and his army were spoken of with contempt and General Wavell's spectacular successes against them were accepted as quite natural, good, but only to be expected.[81]

After a year and a half of war, the food in Ulster is ample. There has been of course a shortage of sugar and fresh fruit. Eggs have been 3/3 a doz. in the second winter of the war but I remember paying 5d each for them in France during the last war. In England the shortage has been rather more acute, eggs I believe in some places very difficult to get and even the correct ration of meat unobtainable.

Spring 1940 was succeeded here by a wretched summer. After a lovely May and a fair June, we had no sun which was strange as in England they had a beautiful summer. Our 'guests' were moved to Bangor, to start a new hospital and I'm afraid none of us regretted them. I had a week's leave and went to Ballynahinch Hotel with Mother and Dorothy but it rained every day and was over all too soon.

---

[81] Field Marshal A. P. Wavell (1883–1950) was Commander-in-Chief Middle East, in which role he led British forces to victory over the Italians in Egypt and Libya in December 1940, only to be defeated by the German army in the western desert in April 1941.

Miss Miller had my room all spring cleaned and gave me such a nice welcome back it warmed my heart to her. She loved the place and when the weather was fine we sauntered round the grounds and she told me of all the different countries she had seen and her many experiences. She was very good company. In the evening she came to my room and I went to hers. I taught her to play French patience and bezique and she insisted on playing every evening.

We got a new sgt major, an objectionable little man who, as the col. said, looked as if he had a bad smell under his nose. He and Miss Miller had many a tussle in which she generally emerged victorious. I also came across him with regard to the V.A.D.s as I found he wanted to treat them like his orderlies, and I would not have it.

I felt I really hadn't quite enough to do, and said so, often to Miss Miller. She chuckled and said 'Neither have I. It's because we're good organisers'. There was a certain amount of truth in this as I was amazed at the muddles and the lack of method in the hospital offices etc. It was extraordinary how one had to struggle for the most obvious necessities. Someone in the quartermaster's office would forget to order the rations and I would pursue inquiries from one source to another. The q.m sergt said he hadn't got the order. The clerk said he had posted the order to the N.A.A.F.I. The clerk in the coy office said he had sent it back because it was wrongly addressed. The sergt said it had never come back to him: net result, no food. An appeal to the quartermaster, hurried, but incompetent telephone messages, complaints, the poor little cooks distracted. Such an unnecessary worry, one that I could have adjusted in five minutes had it not been necessary to pass it though the proper lines of communication. I know the q.m dreaded my approach and one orderly said he never saw me without thinking of washing soda which I had vainly appealed for weeks. Miss Miller took the law into her own hands when she found the water for tea for over 50 people was being boiled in a series of small saucepans.

Autumn succeeded summer. We had a few air raid warnings and orders and counter orders regarding them. We got yellow, purple and red warnings. At first we were to proceed to the kitchen at Stranmillis House on yellow, then it was changed to purple and finally to red. I led my V.A.D.s, protesting, up as I felt as their officer I must see these orders were obeyed but the sisters remained 'put' and I'm sure felt I was fussy. The sgt major got all the orderlies out of bed on every occasion and they marched down with a great clatter of boots and to the accompaniment of shouted orders which roused all the patients and the indignation of the night sisters.

I made each V.A.D. take a blanket, gas mask and torch. They should have had official gas masks and steel helmets and identity discs but these were not issued till months later. I made my Sgt Dispenser and Sgt Cook responsible to see that all bedrooms were vacated. Miss Miller made no secret of hating the alarms and said it gave her a pain when she heard the warning but she did not show outward signs. Miss Luxton got busy and fussy and irritated everyone. Miss McGeary thrived on any form of excitement and revelled in relating Miss Luxton's reaction. They acted like sand paper on each other's nerves.

One afternoon the col. telephoned Miss Miller that her orders were through for her to report at Leeds. She was terribly sorry to go and pulled wires in vain to be allowed to stay. I was very sorry to see her depart. I had got fond of her. She had just been given a present of a canary and bore it off with her. Two sisters who travelled with her reported 'A brigadier who had been a patient at 'Officers' was last seen carrying it for her'. She sat at Leeds for three months, doing nothing. The new Matron did not come for ten days and meanwhile Miss Luxton, as senior sister, officiated, rubbing everyone's back up and changing things for the sake of changing and exercising her power. She made herself and everyone unhappy and Miss McGeary and she were at daggers drawn.

Miss Laver, the new Matron, was rather like an Indian in appearance; in fact everyone openly hinted she was a Eurasian. She was a very nice woman, super conscientious but lacking I think Miss Miller's humour and sense of proportion. I found her pleasant to work with and she took a great interest in my V.A.D.s. She was not such an 'old soldier' as Miss Miller and took refusals by the sgt major and rebuffs by the colonel to see her point too much to heart.

Orders came through for Miss McGeary and another regular, a little Scotch sister, Miss Spence. Both were delighted to go, though the former was sorry she was to go before Xmas as she as Home Sister had made great preparations but they had made up their minds they were going East and were suitably thrilled. We had had a dance in the sisters' mess before that, very well organised by Miss McGeary, who had a flair for that sort of thing., It was marred by the night orderly reporting that the night sister who had been given permission to attend the dance had been drunk and sat in the bunk till 5 in the morning with an officer. Unfortunately, one of my V.A.D.s confirmed this statement and there was inevitably a great deal of talk. Matron was in despair about it all. Fortunately, there had been no intoxicating drinks at the dance and Miss Luxton had seen her go in sober. I had to get the V.A.D. to make a written statement and it was all most unpleasant. I had never liked this sister and she and another had undoubtedly taken too much at a farewell sherry party given by the officers to Miss Miller in the sisters' mess. I thought they would have had her moved but after lectures by the col. and A.D.M.S. she was let off with a warning. Perhaps as well, yet the chief reason given was that an orderly and ward master could not report a ward sister and should have called the orderly M.O. As the D.M.O. that evening was Dr B. who himself got slated at sherry parties I felt sure he would have covered [for] her anyway. After a time the scandal died down but Miss Laver (Matron) decreed that the Xmas dinner was to be purely female and only cider was to be served, as a precaution.

We had our Xmas dinner before Miss McGeary and Miss Spence left so as to combine a farewell to them. If Hitler could have seen that dinner it would have depressed him. We had turkey, sausages, soup, Brussels sprouts, plum pudding and sauce with brandy, mince pies. Not bad for the second Xmas of the war. Little Miss Spence was very Scotch, very strict with the V.A.D.s, suffered from asthma and rarely came to supper, which worried me but Miss McGeary assumed she had suffered with it all her life and she was all right so we were very shocked to hear that, shortly after she left (to Oxford, incidentally, not abroad) she had a bad haemorrhage of the lungs. I am afraid she must have realized her illness was more than asthma, but in my experience trained nurses show less common sense about simple ailments than untrained and seemed to regard the taking of a temperature as fussy.

Christmas came and everyone was very busy, the nurses in hospital, I in the quarters. Miss Laver did not replace Miss McGeary in the House and asked me to carry on, so it fell to me to decorate the quarters, see to the maids' dinner, help Miss Laver with a tea for visitors in the hospital and make preparations for the V.A.D.s' Xmas dinner which did not take place till two days later. I bought an embroider[ed] handkerchief and small calendar for each V.A.D. and tied them up in fancy paper etc.

Miss Coey, one of the cooks, had given a Xmas tree from her garden and poor Miss Spence's 'boyfriend', had had it delivered in a lorry. I had to decorate the tree and rooms unaided as all the V.A.D.s were busy doing the wards.

The hospital looked wonderful. The patients revelled in Xmas trees, paper flowers etc. The night before the V.A.D.s and sisters, augmented by orderlies and one or two outsiders went round the wards singing carols and carrying very pretty bell-shaped lights lent by the Royal Victoria hospital. Miss O'Donnell, one of the cooks who had been a music teacher, was a bad cook but came in useful for the carols, training the singers as choir practices were hard and playing a portable organ she had borrowed.

I was glad when Xmas was over. The V.A.D.s' dinner was a great success. I got a voluntary cook to come and cook it so that the two little lady cooks could enjoy it too. The girls had subscribed to buy a turkey as the official issue was pork. They too had plum pudding and mince pies and the sisters' mess treated them to cider. Miss Laver gave the presents off the tree. Everyone had provided one small present and there were the ones from me too. I dined at home on Xmas night. Harry and Celia called for me and Edmund, D. and the boy came up from Craigavad after dinner.[82] How many similar Xmases had we had. Would we have another?

Ruth suddenly got warning that the Riddel Hall was to be taken for the ATS and she had to turn out, which caused a great turmoil[83]. Enormous brick walls were built outside the windows to protect them from blast, which amused us as we had no protection at our quarters. In the end the ATS did not take it over and after all the fuss and a lot of expense the students returned, but not till Easter.

Meanwhile many people had their houses taken or soldiers billeted in them. Lady Clanwilliam was still allowed to keep a wing at Montalto and was delighted as the military had connected her up with the official electricity scheme and water which she could not previously afford.[84] Lady Mabel Annesley, less lucky, was turned out at a moment's notice, all

---

[82] Edmund was the elder of Emma's two brothers.

[83] Emma's sister Ruth was principal at Riddel Hall from 1914 to 1943.

[84] Lady Clanwilliam, Montalto House, Co. Down. Muriel Mary Temple Stephenson (1876–1952) born in Canada, married Arthur Vesey Meade, 5th Earl of Clanwilliam in 1909.

The lawns at Queen's University Belfast, May 1944, adapted for use as vegetable plots to assist in the 'Dig for Victory' campaign.

her valuable books and pictures being carried down to the cellars by Tommies. Poor Una Ross heard that Peter had been lost with his ship. The casualty lists were published, as in the last war. One got very little news, except on the wireless, which seemed constantly repeated and appeared again [in] the newspapers. A shortage of paper made itself felt and the newspapers shrank. Small shops began to disappear. Rationing became stricter. Such things as marmalade and all foreign fruit, bananas, oranges etc, became unattainable but the standard of food still remained wonderfully good. One got rather tired of sausages and bored with re-iterated directions on the wireless to eat carrots and potatoes.

The wireless was chiefly propaganda or music hall or news endlessly repeated and re-served. Of course the difficulties of the BBC must have been enormous and the foreign broadcasts in every tongue difficult to keep up. But the results for the ordinary listeners were certainly disappointing. We still had the democratic right to criticise but more and more of the democratic rights were of necessity disappearing.

Milk bottle tops and ration book

At the beginning of Jan. [1941] I got leave and went to spend it with Celia, who was very glad to have me as Harry had had to go to London for a few days. It was lovely to be free, to have morning tea and late breakfast and to do what one wanted. But leave was clouded by dear Scrabo's death.[85] He had been seedy for some

NIWM Collection

85 The family dog, *Scrabo*, was a spaniel.

time and the vet had to pronounce his death sentence. Poor Dorothy was broken-hearted. We missed him at every turn: when I went home I instinctively looked for his greeting, his friendly wriggles, his endearing black nose poked into my hand. He had an easy death compared to the deaths being suffered by humans in every quarter of the globe. We shrank from horrors, hoped they were not all true. I was sick of pictures in the *Illustrated London News*, of guns, battleships, aeroplanes and still more guns. *John O'London's Weekly* still kept its quiet, literary character but otherwise one paper was like another. Bernard Partridge faded out of *Punch* and there seemed nobody to replace him as a cartoonist.[86] Shepherd, who could draw dainty illustrations for 'Ballads' and 'Phantasies', seemed to me in style quite unsuited as a cartoonist.[87] Most of the drawings were wretched little scribbles which, even if occasionally clever, would have taken neither skill of penmanship nor time to produce. I felt old-fashioned, I longed for Townshend[88], Partridge, Ravenhill[89] even du Maurier[90] of long ago days. I was out of touch and sympathy with the modern poetry and art and turned to the literature and art of old, peaceful, quiet, leisured times. Mamma took to reading Trollope out loud to Dorothy.

One could not go to the pictures without seeing and hearing horror. Molly and I came out in the middle of Pastor Hall, the story (reputed to be) of Pastor Nichmöller in Germany, in which the worst atrocities of the German prison camps were depicted, nothing being left to the imagination.[91] We were horrified to see children watching it. What will be the result on the next generation? Will they be frightened, nervy, haunted or callous, cruel, blind to the suffering of their fellow men?

Miss Miller, before she left, had set two balls rolling, one a hospital for the women's services at Stranmillis, in the same building as the officers, the

[86] Sir Bernard Partridge (1861–1945) book and poster illustrator was principal cartoonist with *Punch* in the first quarter of the 20th century.

[87] *Phantasies* is the name of a series of animated cartoons produced for Columbia Pictures 1939–46, the last theatrical animated series produced in black and white.

[88] G. K. Townshend (1888–1969) New Zealand-born illustrator and cartoonist.

[89] Leonard Raven-Hill (1867–1942) artist and illustrator had also worked on *Punch*.

[90] George du Maurier (1834–1896) was a French-born cartoonist who had worked on *Punch* in the nineteenth century. (He was also the father of novelist Daphne du Maurier.)

[91] *Pastor Hall* was a 1940 British film directed by Roy Boulting which told the story of a young German man sent to Dachau concentration camp for criticising the Nazi party.

other a shelter for V.A.D.s and the sisters between the bungalow at the quarters. It took months for these two plans to be carried into effect but they eventually were. We had been threatened for many months that an inventory of equipment in the hospital and quarters were (sic) to be taken. I must say I had been absolutely amazed at the quarters that I had never been given one. Rumour said £1000 worth of equipment had disappeared. Mr Warren, a cocky little cockney who had succeeded Capt V. as Q.M. hinted at court materials, courts of enquiries etc while Capt V. (now Q.M. of the Command stores) looked balefully at him and lost weight visibly. At last the day of reckoning came. Miss Laver asked me, as she had no Home sister, if I would do the inventory and I couldn't well refuse. But oh, what a job! 100 bedrooms and silver, floors etc in proportion. The servants worked like blacks,[92] counting spoons, chasing missing knives pursuing lost blankets and sheets. We worked at it for three solid days, Mr Warren, the staff sgt and I parading round, the maids running hither and thither completely mystified by the strange names given to the kitchen utensils. It was extraordinarily badly done but at last was accomplished. Mr Warren and I 'foundered' with the cold as every bedroom in the place had its window open!

On the last day I had been told that 2 V.A.D.s were being transferred from Holywood. I had with difficulty accomplished getting their beds made and rooms ready. Imagine my feelings when one mentioned casually that 9 more were to arrive that afternoon. We were all utterly exhausted with equipment. I had no rations for them and there was no possibility owing to difficulties of transport of getting any delivered for 2 to 5 days. Insane! I got Matron on the telephone who said she would have them stopped but the colonel, manlike, could not appreciate our difficulties and refused to take any steps. They arrived, plus a couple of suitcases each, and somehow we had to cope with them. They had come, we were informed, to get ready the new women's hospital but owing to the fact that the equipment there, and in Officers, was being taken the following day, they could not be supplied with a brush or a duster. Add to this the dull January days and not one electric bulb forthcoming and the folly of it will be appreciated.

What was to have prevented Holywood ringing Matron and asking what day she would be ready for them and time given to order rations, I do not

---

[92] With a view to keeping the transcription as faithful to the original as possible, it has been decided to retain this otherwise unacceptable phrase.

66

know. If they had come from Dunkirk it might have been excusable; as it was, it was the usual British army muddle. The girls themselves had been given a couple of hours' notice; their commandant had never been officially informed at all. Some of them had been snatched off night duty and had no sleep. Again, I say, inexcusable! I had seen it and suffered it in the last war. Here it was again. Bad organisation always irritates me. Somehow, the women's hospital did get opened and patients were admitted, though weeks later I heard it had not yet been approved by the W.O. and therefore we had no official staff, hence the Holywood V.A.D.s attached for temporary duty.

A few weeks later Miss Laver got orders to report to Hatfield and Miss Luxton to Woolwich. Both were most unwilling to go, partly that they considered Belfast as safe, though as things turned out later it was far from being so. Miss Davey, the next senior sister, was to act as Matron till the new one arrived. To my horror, Miss Laver proposed that she should sign for the equipment in the quarters and she refused to do unless she had checked them personally. I refused to take anything more to do with it and Miss Davey and a V.A.D. made a half-hearted effort to count the stores and cutlery and blankets but were daunted by the immensity of the task and she signed, registering a protest and declaring she would not be responsible. She had all my sympathy.

A day or two later, Miss McC [name scribbled out], the new Matron, arrived. She was a contrast to Miss Laver. She had little kiss curls showing below her cap, not bad eyes, a good complexion, and a pleasant manner when pleased and most unpleasant as I learnt later when not pleased. Miss Davey, who had known her before, reported her to [have] been constantly ill and she had just come from sick leave after bronchitis. She had been at the Duke of Richmond's at Goodwood as Matron and obviously the ducal entourage had pleased her and our quarters, though we considered them fairly comfortable, struck her as cold and draughty, which they certainly were. She took no interest in V.A.D.s, unlike Miss Laver and Miss Miller, and it was obvious from the first that, cat-like, if we saved her trouble she would purr, but if we bothered her she would spit.

She took no trouble to know the girls, was unsympathetic towards any requests – reports of minor ills, took them off and on night duty at a moment's notice as if they were pawns in a game. When I asked a question I was always told 'Later. I will see to it. Ask me again'. But I never got an answer.

A girl might be waiting to catch a train but Matron would not make time to sign a pass. What a contrast to Miss Miller who would have come running up the hill with it herself had I not been there. I had acknowledged Red X gifts to oblige the two former Matrons. It was now taken for granted that she did not acknowledge any, though she might occasionally sign one of my letters if I thought it advisable to ask her.

This made my job much more difficult. More orderlies were called away and we got 13 new V.A.D.s. Raw recruits. This brought my numbers up to 51 and the A.D.M.S. had also appointed me commandant to the girls at Donegall Rd hospital so I was kept quite busy. I filled 160 forms for the 13 new V.A.D.s alone! Identity cards, pay books, forms in duplicate, in triplicate etc etc etc. Lists to be made for inoc[ulation] vacc[ination], gas masks, steel helmets, Med. Exams: Matron made it all difficult. She blocked efforts to get the med. examined. They couldn't be spared. If I asked when they could, I was put off. I was perpetually told to tell my V.A.D.s not to do this, not to do that, to make less noise. I found her unapproachable: I could never discuss points with her. She gave me 5 minutes' notice to give the V.A.D.s instructions on some point which, as there were now 51 of them, was impossible.

4 BELFAST AIR RAIDS APRIL–MAY 1941

Although Emma notes that Belfast had been 'singularly free from air raid warnings' that all changed when 'On Tuesday April 15 41 I was awakened by the sirens at 10. 45'. The aerial attack that night would account for almost 800 fatalities, the great majority of them civilian. Curiously, the focus of the attack was on the north of the city. Emma, superintending her VAD charges as they sheltered throughout that long night on the south side of the city, describes the crescendo of noise and frightening impact of flames. 'We realized this was a real 'Blitz' but not till the next day did we know how severe it had been'.

Most gripping of all is the eye-witness account of the aftermath of the blitz as she made the journey across the bomb-cratered city to give a first aid talk in stricken north Belfast that had previously been arranged and which, she was told in spite of everything, had to go ahead. She travels, on foot or in a car, through quarters of the city centre and via Carlisle Circus up the Antrim and Oldpark Roads. There is an almost eerie sense of calm after the storm as the transport system, or what was left of it, struggled to maintain a service. Even the evacuation of families stricken or left homeless seemed to be undertaken in a calm, if shocked, orderliness. Just as poignantly, Emma later remembers to look for two elderly unmarried sisters, family friends, in Sheridan Street, near Carlisle Circus, only to find the house utterly destroyed and reduced to dust. She does not mention it but the two Misses Addis had in fact been killed (their names feature on the Commonwealth War Graves Commission list of dead in Belfast that night).

Emma's already stressful week finishes with a harrowing stint at St George's Market, where unidentified bodies had been laid out. Her role is to accompany families in their sometimes forlorn search for missing family members. After her slightly incongruous observation 'Will I ever bring myself to buy flowers and vegetables there again?' Emma describes in harrowing detail what was involved, for her and the unfortunate family members, as they continued their grisly searches. 'I came away drawing deep breaths of fresh air', she recalls. 'So this was the result of a Blitz. I prayed I would never see it again'. In fact there was another heavy Luftwaffe attack on the city three weeks later but with considerably fewer civilian fatalities and less impact on housing sectors, the damage being mostly confined to the city's manufacturing and industrial sectors. Nonetheless, these two raids resulted in 1,000 deaths.

PRONI D3119/2/4

Air Raids

Ring up 28211 – 2 8 4

WARDEN'S REPORT FORM. A.R.P./M.I.

Form of Report to Report Centres.

(Commence with the words)   "AIR RAID DAMAGE"

Designation of REPORTING AGENT (e.g., Warden's Sector Number)   *Riddel Hall Sector. Group M. District F*

POSITION of occurrence

TYPE of bombs :—H.E.   Incendiary   Poison Gas

Approx. No. of CASUALTIES :— (If any trapped under wreckage, say so)

If FIRE say so :—

Damage to MAINS :—Water   Coal Gas   Overhead electric cables   Sewers

Names of ROADS BLOCKED

Position of any UNEXPLODED BOMBS

Time of occurrence (approx.) *(use 24 hour clock . e.g. 9.15 = 21.15)*

Services already ON THE SPOT or COMING :—

Remarks :—

(Finish with the words)   "MESSAGE ENDS"

ORIGINAL DUPLICATE } These words are for use with a report sent by messenger. Delete whichever does not apply.

Air Raid Warden's Report Form, Riddel Hall, Belfast

Belfast Telegraph

Salvage work at Ballyclare Street. Emma travelled across the devastated city two days after the Blitz, to give a first-aid lecture to the Women's Voluntary Service (WVS) in the Oldpark area, close to Ballyclare Street

diary pages 87–111

We had been singularly free from air raid warnings beyond an occasional yellow until April 1941.[93] Then one night the sirens hooted. I got my V.A.D.s out and herded them unwillingly in to the new shelter. It was dripping with damp and a cold chill struck through one's bones but the anti-aircraft guns were firing and the sound of bombs dropping in the distance made me refuse piteous requests to be allowed to go back to bed. We spent most of the night in the shelter and the next day I begged permission to take them to the kitchen of 'officers' again if there should be another raid. Little damage had been done in this one but our turn was to come.

On Tuesday April 15 [19]41 I was awakened by the sirens at 10.45 and almost instantaneously the anti-aircraft guns roared out.[94] I hustled into my clothes and ran down the corridor to see that the girls were all awake and dressing and that all black outs were up. I turned off the electricity at the base every night so that there was no possibility of maybe switching on an uncovered light. The barrage grew more intense and the girls seemed to me incredibly slow about dressing but dressing by torchlight with rather trembling fingers is not easy. At last the sergeants and I had assured ourselves that all bedrooms were empty and we followed the rest up to the kitchen and half underground passages of Stranmillis House 'Officers'. It was an old-fashioned, well-built, stone house and the kitchen had steel beams across the ceiling which was rather reassuring.

The girls soon settled down. Some lay on shelves, others on tables or the floor, wrapped in their blankets. The day sisters had gone on duty but the V.A.D.s' instructions were to wait for orders. They were bringing the patients down from the top floor and presently the up-patients from the women's wards were sent down to us. We made them as comfortable as we could. To my surprise, Matron remained with us. I had thought her place would have been in the main hospital. I could have well done without her as she was very fussy. She refused to let us have any light; although the black-outs were up, as she said, they fitted badly. She was,

---

[93] The first raid over Belfast was on the night of 7–8 April 1941, when, Brian Barton says in *The Belfast Blitz. The City in the War Years* (Belfast, 2015) p. 132 'the final casualty figure was thirteen dead … [and] over eighty persons … injured.'

[94] Brian Barton, *op. cit.*, p. 157, confirms the intensity of the raid on 15–16 April described by Emma. 'Luftwaffe records indicate that … their aircraft dropped 750 bombs' from the estimated 180 German planes. The great majority fell on the northern part of the city, away from Stranmillis in the south.

I must admit, right there, for I could see the light of the flares the German planes were dropping through the cracks. On the other hand, it was a beautiful moonlit night and as light as day outside.

I speculated that if any of the girls got hysterical or nervy, sitting in the dark would not be good for morale yet if one even put on a small pocket torch to look at a watch she called out to them to extinguish it. Meanwhile the noise of the barrage and the thud of falling bombs continued. We realized this was a real 'Blitz' but not till the next day did we know how severe it had been. Some of the girls went to sleep and snored loudly. Others talked almost incessantly. One of the newly-joined, a French girl, married to an English husband, chattered all the time but none showed signs of nerves and the maids too behaved very well. Owing to the dark I could not see that everyone was there but knew nobody had been left in the quarters. There were slight pauses but not of long duration. I sat on a kitchen chair, glad of the eiderdown I had brought, with my steel helmet on and my gas mask on my shoulders. I would much rather have been on duty. The night seemed interminable. It was not till nearly 6am that we heard the welcome sound of the 'all clear'. When we emerged we saw the sky red with the reflection from fires and realized there must be a good deal of damage. One of the girls reported that 2 V.A.D.s whose train had been due in at 11pm had not come back. I hoped it had stopped outside Belfast but could make no inquiries till later.

Everyone went on duty as usual next day. We learnt that several incendiary bombs had fallen in the hospital grounds and on the Stranmillis Road. The milkman brought news of objectives which had been hit. Girls whose people were in vulnerable areas were anxious and tore off in their off-duty time to learn the extent of the damage. Two of them and two of the kitchen maids had had their homes demolished but their people were safe. One girl came back with a green face and her eyes like saucers. Her home was gone, her people at a rest centre but she had seen the dead body of a child carried from the ruins of a house and it had shaken her. Bit by bit news of the extensive damage reached us. Harland and Wolff's, Victoria Barracks, Ewart's mill, Dixon's timber yard. Some reports were exaggerated but it was obvious a good deal of damage had been done. At 11 o'clock my 2 girls turned up, one very shaky. They had spent the night on the train which, as I had hoped, had stopped at Whitehead and had not run into Belfast.

We got few casualties, most of them going to the civilian hospitals which were very full. I went to the Donegall Rd Military Hospital to see how my V.A.D.s there had stood it. I stopped first at the billets and saw the lady cook. She was a very young girl and had been left alone in the house with some young maids as the sisters had all gone on duty. She seemed to have stood it well but said she would have liked a steel helmet. One of the maids had been badly scared. There was no shelter and they had stayed in the hall. Some of the V.A.D.s had been left in the other part of the quarters on the opposite side of the road and the cook reported one had been badly scared so I proceeded to the hospital to inquire. The hospital was really a wing of the Infirmary and one passed through the workhouse gates to reach it. At the gate was a lorry and I learnt later it had brought the dead bodies to the Infirmary mortuary and some of the V.A.D.s had been upset by seeing them brought in. I first saw the little clerk who I heard had been very nervy. She came from Eire. 'Oh Miss Duffin', she said, 'there's no good saying anything but that I was a coward. I was terribly scared. I am going on leave next week and I doubt if I can ever come back'. I talked cheerily to her and tried to steady her and told her she must not let down the Red X and I was sure she wouldn't desert the army. The quartermaster, who was also co[mpan]y officer, was nice about it and said he thought it had been too trying leaving them alone and he was arranging if there was another Blitz to send a cpl and a pte from a unit billeted near to fire watch and give the girls confidence.

I talked to several of the other girls who looked tired but calm but one poor child, who also came from Eire, looked dazed and shaken. 'I don't really know what I'm doing', she said, 'and the sister on the ward has been re-called to another hospital where there are casualties. Oh I am glad to see you'. 'You'll have to keep calm if sister's gone. They'll depend on you' I said, but I felt a bit worried about her. She had been ill recently and a very agitated and fussy mother had arrived from Queen's County.[95]

[95] Queen's County in the midlands of Ireland was re-named *Laois* following Partition.

The primary target of the Luftwaffe, the Harland & Wolff shipyard, sustained considerable damage in the second major air raid of 4–5 May 1941

With the permission of Harland & Wolff and The Deputy Keeper of the Records, PRONI D2805/PHT/B/6

She referred to her always as 'Bubbles' and spoke of how marvellous 'Bubbles' had been in the air raids at Bristol and what a wonderful nurse she was. Actually, she was unsuited to be a nurse as she was untidy and messy and never got good reports though she was a nice child to speak to and meant well. I began to wonder whether poor 'Bubbles' had stood up to the air raids in Bristol as well as her fond mother imagined. She was going to our house to tea the next day so I slipped round after tea to see how she was. She still looked dazed and her clothes were put on any way. Her shoes were filthy and even her hands looked dirty. She told me she had felt cold and shivery ever since the Blitz so as she had a ½ day I advised her to go to bed with a hot drink and a hot water bag.

The offices of the daily evening newspaper, the *Belfast Telegraph*, which, although damaged in the April air raid, continued to publish

Belfast Telegraph

NIWM Collection

Women's Voluntary Services badge. The WVS had been founded in 1938 by the Marchioness of Reading to encourage women to help with air raid precautions

The next day I had promised to give a 1st aid lecture, one of a course of 4, to a class organised by the Women's Voluntary Service at a school in the top of the Oldpark Road.[96] I asked would I still be required and was told 'yes', to carry on. I knew the tram service was dislocated so left myself plenty of time, as I thought, but I soon realized I would be very late. Town was crowded, chiefly with people wanting to see the damage. The centre was all right but when I reached Royal Avenue I saw a crater in the road and the Free Library was pitted all over and shop people were busy boarding up their windows on both sides of the road.[97]

---

[96] Likely to have been Finiston Public Elementary School at 383 Oldpark Road.

[97] Belfast Central Library in Royal Avenue.

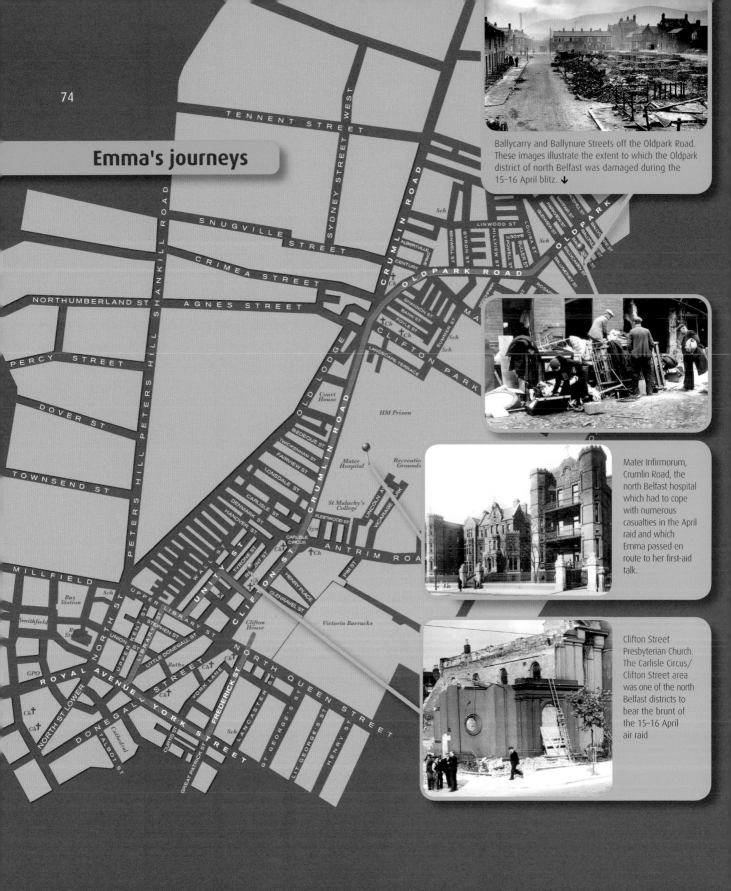

Ballycarry and Ballynure Streets off the Oldpark Road. These images illustrate the extent to which the Oldpark district of north Belfast was damaged during the 15–16 April blitz. ↓

Mater Infirmorum, Crumlin Road, the north Belfast hospital which had to cope with numerous casualties in the April raid and which Emma passed en route to her first-aid talk.

Clifton Street Presbyterian Church. The Carlisle Circus/ Clifton Street area was one of the north Belfast districts to bear the brunt of the 15–16 April air raid

74

Emma's journeys

TENNENT STREET WEST

SYDNEY STREET WEST

SNUGVILLE STREET

CRIMEA STREET

SHANKILL ROAD

NORTHUMBERLAND ST

AGNES STREET

PETERS HILL

PERCY STREET

DOVER ST

TOWNSEND STREET

MILLFIELD

CRUMLIN ROAD

OLDPARK ROAD

LINWOOD ST

BENWELL ST

BYRON ST

HILLVIEW ST

LOUISA ST

BULLER ST

ALBERTVILLE DRIVE

CENTURY

SHANNON ST

BANN ST

ROYLE ST

SUMMER ST

CLIFTON PARK

LANDSCAPE TERRACE

Sch
Sch
Sch
Ch
Ch

MCNEILL ST
MAYFAIR ST
HARVEY ST
GLENVIEW ST
BADEN POWELL ST
RECKPARK ST
BALLYMONEY ST
ROSARY
BALLYNURE ST
BALLYCARRY ST

Sch

OLD LODGE

Court House

HM Prison

Mater Hospital

Recreation Grounds

St Malachy's College

LINCOLN AV

VICARAGE PARK

Syn

BEDEQUE ST

TWICKENHAM ST

FAIRVIEW ST

LONSDALE ST

CARLISLE ST

DENMARK ST

HANOVER ST

CARLISLE CIRCUS

FLEETWOOD ST

Ch†

Ch†

ANTRIM ROAD

PIM ST

HENRY PLACE

GLENRAVEL ST

Victoria Barracks

UNITY ST

WALL ST

TYRONE ST

REGENT ST

CLIFTON ST

UPPER LIBRARY ST

STEPHEN ST

UNION ST

UPPER KENT ST

LIBRARY ST

LITTLE DONEGALL ST

Clifton House

NORTH QUEEN STREET

FREDERICK ST

Baths

Ch†

YORK LANE

Ch†

Ch†

LANCASTER ST

GT GEORGES ST

LIT GEORGES ST

HENRY ST

Bus Station

Sch

Smithfield

Bk St

GPO

ROYAL AVENUE

NORTH ST

DONEGALL ST

YORK STREET

NORTH ST LOWER

Ch†

Ch†

Cathedral

TALBOT ST

GREAT PATRICK ST

CURTIS ST

Sch

I made my way to the tram and finally decided to hail a car. Two men responded to my appeal and though they were going up the Antrim Road they good-naturedly said they'd take me the whole way. They both had what looked like government cases and so I imagined had petrol, so I accepted their offer.

At Carlisle Circus we saw the bank in ruins. I wondered what had happened to the manager and his wife, whom we knew slightly, who lived there. Later we heard they had escaped and taken refuge in the Savings Bank and were bombed out of that too, but again escaped. We passed the Mater hospital where many victims had been taken. The nurses' home had been hit. As we got higher up the road we began to realise the extent of the damage. Little side streets in ruins, houses reduced to dust. We were diverted into another road, not much better. We saw a street shelter which had received a direct hit, killing most of the occupants. The concrete top seemed to have been ripped off. When I arrived at my school, I felt almost a fool to come to speak to householders here on 1st aid. Many to whom I should have spoken would now be beyond the need of 1st aid themselves but having come I made my way into the school. It was intact; so were all its windows. It had been used for the last two days to interview applicants for relief, give temporary assistance, arrange evacuations but it was practically empty and the voluntary workers were snatching a well earned luncheon. Feeling rather foolish, I turned away. There were no trams. In spite of my welcome lift, I had walked a good way already and my gas mask and steel helmet weighed me down but there was nothing for it but to start for home. Buses were running at long intervals but were so crowded there was no hope of a seat. I was joined by a friendly little person who had been a V.A.D. in the last war. She had come to look for a friend but found her gone. We tramped on and presently a woman showed us a short-cut. She told me how she and her mother, a large stout woman, had spent the night under the dining room table. Soon we reached the devastated area.[98] Not a window was left unbroken. Many homes were deserted. Glimpses down side streets showed demolition squads and military digging frantically. Awful to think there might still be people alive in those heaps of rubble. A church was completely gutted yet a plate glass window in the butcher's next to it had not received a crack.

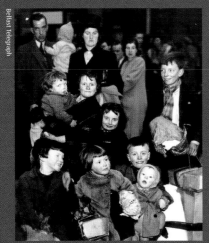

Belfast Telegraph

The Butler family queuing with many others 'bombed out', waiting to be evacuated following the April air raids.

---

[98] The 'devastated area' could have been anywhere from Carlisle Circus in the direction of Crumlin, Oldpark, Cliftonville and Antrim Roads, all parts of north Belfast that had been seriously affected.

76

The badly damaged Salisbury Avenue tramway depot, off the Antrim Road in north Belfast

A policeman stopped his car and took us as far as the nearest trams but the trams were too full to attempt. Everywhere were people with parcels or suitcases, struggling to get away. Who could blame them? We tramped on and at last were offered another lift. I returned to the hospital exhausted but feeling how grateful I should be, that I and all my family and our houses were intact.

I had heard the nurses' home in Frederick Street had been hit and, as I had been on the committee in the pre-war days, I thought I would go round and inquire for the Matron. I started the next afternoon but was unprepared for what I was to see. I passed up York Street where every window in the big Cooperative building was smashed, turned into Frederick Street and saw with horror that only the outside shell of the building was standing. I asked a woman in a small house what had happened to the inmates and was told they were saved and taken to the Friends' meeting house opposite so I went across to inquire. They had moved to the 'Old Charitable' at the top of the street so I proceeded there. It was a dignified old building, the oldest charity in Belfast.[99] Here in old days routs and balls had been held. The board room and offices and hall were filled with old furniture, old prints and many interesting relics. In the front lawn a barrage balloon was tethered. I passed between beds of sweet-smelling wallflowers over which the balloons hovered like some sinister and threatening masters. Here had come old men and women who had toiled through life, to end their days in peace, but Hitler had ordained it otherwise. I found Miss Ellis, the Matron of the home. She looked white and shaken, but calm. It was, she said, incendiary bombs that had damaged the building. She and the asst

---

[99] Clifton House, home of the Belfast Charitable Society, established in the 1770s, which had continued to serve as a home for the care of elderly and worthy Belfast citizens. R. W. M. Strain's *Belfast and its Charitable Society. A Story of Urban Social Development* (Oxford University Press, 1961) p. 313 records that 'When the 1939–45 war broke out it was decided that the cellar storey of the house would make an excellent air raid shelter but on 29 April 1941 the House was evacuated and the residents and staff moved to Garron Tower on the Antrim Coast, the bed-ridden residents being transported by the St John Ambulance Brigade …. The front lawn was used as a site for the balloon barrage of Belfast.'

Glenavel Local History Project (North Belfast)

Clifton House on Clifton Street in north Belfast, built in the 1770s, somehow survived the barrage of bombs that had fallen all around it

Matron had been there alone with the maids. The nurses were all out at cases. It had been a horrible experience. She had lost all her clothes but she was thankful to be safe.

As I returned to hospital, I thought of the meetings I had attended in the home. I had persuaded them to make a garden for the nurses recently. Well, it was not really much loss. It had survived its usefulness. It dated back to the days when it was the first home of its kind in Belfast. *Aunt Dodsie* had been its first Hon. Sec. which was why I had stuck on the committee, first to please her then out of loyalty to her memory.[100] I smiled as I thought of the bad but probably speaking likeness [of a painting] of a former matron or chairwoman which had presided at all the meetings. Her calm, placid, Victorian face, surmounted by a ribbon in her hair, the locket on her breast, her simply folded hands with a delicate lace handkerchief daintily held between her fingers in the ample lap of her full silk dress. Did that calm face show no fear, or only resignation, as the flames shriveled her face and licked her dress, did she drop her handkerchief and hold up her hands in horror that such things could be. Nobody saw her perish but the artist who painted her could never have anticipated that that she should be destroyed by 'enemy action'.

---

[100] *Aunt Dodsie* was the pet name for Emma's aunt Dorothy.

Meanwhile everyone was working very hard, some coping with evacuees at rest centres, feeding and clothing them and then driving them to places of safety. The usual tales were told of the incredible dirt of the people; of children crawling with lice, not even house-trained who destroyed mattresses, stuffed clothes down w.c.s in order to get new ones; of women turning up with naked children who were fully clothed and the same women and the same children turning up at another rest centre the following day, the babies once more naked. All a terrible indictment of our way of life. We heard of wardens leaving their posts, of panic, also of incredible bravery, of hopeless inefficiency in some quarters and quiet, ordered organization in others. I suppose it will always be so. It takes all sorts to make a world.

Molly and Dorothy went to look for poor old Nurse White who lived with a friend in a bad district; also two old women whom Dorothy and Molly had befriended for years, the two old Addis sisters. They found old Nurse White's house completely emptied of furniture and the neighbours said they had gone to the country. Later we heard from the poor old thing, comfortably established on a farm. They had spent the night in a coal cellar but who had evacuated them so successfully with their furniture she did not say.

The old Addis's house was reduced to powder.[101] The neighbours said there was a rumour that one had been taken out alive but it seemed doubtful. Two poor little inoffensive old maids whose chief interest was the goings and comings of the society about them. They had always taken an innocent pleasure in following the careers of our friends and acquaintances. Every 12th July, every Easter, one turned up for flowers. On Easter Monday, Minnie had come as usual, had her gossip, her flowers, her train fare, and had departed, such an unlikely place to die, in the front line, facing Hitler. Yet thousands like her had gone the same way. 20,000 dead in Belgrade, 30,000 in Rotterdam. How can that man face death when it comes to him. Is it possible that he cannot be haunted by the cries and moans of the innocent victims, in his own country and all over Europe. Was any human being ever before responsible for so much misery?

---

[101] *Belfast Directory* 1941 p.524 records 'Sarah Addis' as being resident at 23 Sheridan Street. Sheridan Street was situated off the Antrim Road near Carlisle Circus, a particularly devastated part of the city. The Commonwealth War Graves Commission list of fatalities, 'by far the most comprehensive and accurate ever compiled', maintains Brian Barton, includes 'Mary Addis, aged 59 of 23 Sheridan Street' and 'Sarah Addis aged 64' among its 900 names. The list is helpfully reproduced in Barton *Belfast Blitz* pp573–621.

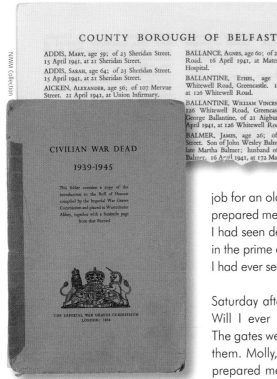

COUNTY BOROUGH OF BELFAST

ADDIS, MARY, age 59; of 23 Sheridan Street. 15 April 1941, at 21 Sheridan Street.

ADDIS, SARAH, age 64; of 23 Sheridan Street. 15 April 1941, at 21 Sheridan Street.

AICKEN, ALEXANDER, age 56; of 107 Mervue Street. 21 April 1941, at Union Infirmary.

BALLANCE, AGNES, age 60; of 24 Mt. Collyer Road. 16 April 1941, at Mater Infirmorum Hospital.

BALLANTINE, ETHEL, age 27; of 126 Whitewell Road, Greencastle. 16 April 1941, at 126 Whitewell Road.

BALLANTINE, WILLIAM VINCENT, age 30; of 126 Whitewell Road, Greencastle. Son of George Ballantine, of 21 Aigburth Park. 16 April 1941, at 126 Whitewell Road.

BALMER, JAMES, age 26; of 172 Manor Street. Son of John Wesley Balmer, and of the late Martha Balmer; husband of Edith Maud Balmer. 16 April 1941, at 172 Manor Street.

CIVILIAN WAR DEAD
1939-1945

This folder contains a copy of the introduction to the Roll of Honour, compiled by the Imperial War Graves Commission and placed in Westminster Abbey, together with a facsimile page from that Record

THE IMPERIAL WAR GRAVES COMMISSION
LONDON: 1954

The Commonwealth War Graves Commission Civilian War Dead Roll of Honour, in which feature the two elderly Addis sisters, Sheridan Street, who Emma knew well.

Poor Molly was exhausted working with the St John people, at evacuations, 1st aid parties etc etc. I told her I would fill any gaps as my time at hospital was by no means fully occupied and I felt it was the civilians who needed help. She asked me would I mind going on duty at the markets where the relations came to search for their dead amongst the unidentified bodies. Of course I said I would, though nobody could not but have dreaded it. Still, it was a job for an older woman and my former experience in hospital should have prepared me to a certain extent for the sight of death. I say should have, but I had seen death in many forms, young boys dying of ghastly wounds, men in the prime of life dying by inches of dysentery or septicaemia, but nothing I had ever seen was as terrible as this.

Saturday afternoon, the fifth day after the Blitz, I went to the market.[102] Will I ever bring myself to buy flowers and vegetables there again? The gates were guarded by police. But at sight of my uniform they opened them. Molly, poor thing, had already been there and to a certain extent prepared me for what I was to see. The place was full of coffins, some varnished but the majority plain deal. At the end of the hall was a Salvation Army mobile canteen. And beside it was a rough table where some men with papers took particulars. Red X and St John nurses and some civilian volunteers met and went round with the relatives. Two men went round with each group and opened the coffins, lifting the lids. There were two doctors in attendance. A man watered the ground with disinfectant from a watering pot, a wise precaution as the place smelt. It was a lofty airy place, fortunately, but a bitter cold wind swept through the gates and the disinfectant had soaked and made puddles on the floor.[103] It was a hideous nightmare. Only small groups were allowed in at a time, mercifully. I went with a man and his wife first. They looked desolate, exhausted, with red-rimmed eyes and haggard faces. They were looking for a sister-in-law. They had seen all these coffins but more were being brought in and they hung round waiting.

---

[102] St George's Market, constructed in the 1890s in the 'Markets' area of the city, was and is best known for fresh fruit and vegetables.

[103] PRONI MPS/2/3/99 contains information regarding procedures to be followed at St George's Market in the event of enemy action, and a list of the dead identified there in April 1941.

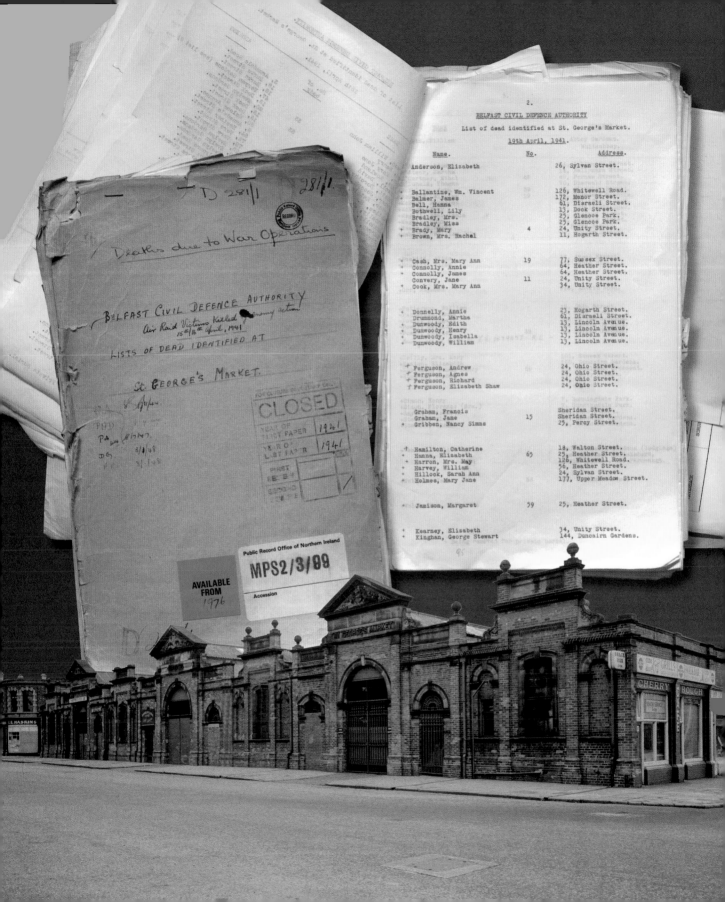

Deaths due to War Operations

BELFAST CIVIL DEFENCE AUTHORITY
Air Raid Victims killed by enemy action
15th/16th April, 1941

LISTS OF DEAD IDENTIFIED AT

St. GEORGE'S MARKET.

CLOSED
YEAR OF FIRST PAPER 1941
YEAR OF LAST PAPER 1941

2.

BELFAST CIVIL DEFENCE AUTHORITY

List of dead identified at St. George's Market.

19th April, 1941.

Name.	No.	Address.
Anderson, Elizabeth		26, Sylvan Street.
Ballantine, Wm. Vincent		126, Whitewell Road.
Balmer, James		172, Manor Street.
Bell, Hanna		64, Disraeli Street.
Bothwell, Lily		13, Dock Street.
Bradley, Mrs.		25, Glencoe Park.
Bradley, Miss		25, Glencoe Park.
Brady, Mary	4	24, Unity Street.
Brown, Mrs. Rachel		11, Hogarth Street.
Cash, Mrs. Mary Ann	19	77, Sussex Street.
Connolly, Annie		64, Heather Street.
Connolly, James		64, Heather Street.
Convery, Jane	11	24, Unity Street.
Cook, Mrs. Mary Ann		34, Unity Street.
Donnelly, Annie		23, Hogarth Street.
Drummond, Martha		61, Disraeli Street.
Dunwoody, Edith		13, Lincoln Avenue.
Dunwoody, Henry		13, Lincoln Avenue.
Dunwoody, Isabella		13, Lincoln Avenue.
Dunwoody, William		13, Lincoln Avenue.
Ferguson, Andrew		24, Ohio Street.
Ferguson, Agnes		24, Ohio Street.
Ferguson, Richard		24, Ohio Street.
Ferguson, Elizabeth Shaw		24, Ohio Street.
Graham, Francis		Sheridan Street.
Graham, Jane	15	Sheridan Street.
Gribben, Nancy Simms		25, Percy Street.
Hamilton, Catherine		18, Walton Street.
Hanna, Elizabeth	65	25, Heather Street.
Harron, Mrs. May		126, Whitewell Road.
Harvey, William		56, Heather Street.
Hillock, Sarah Ann		24, Sylvan Street.
Holmes, Mary Jane		177, Upper Meadow Street.
Jamison, Margaret	59	25, Heather Street.
Kearney, Elizabeth		34, Unity Street.
Kinghan, George Stewart		144, Duncairn Gardens.

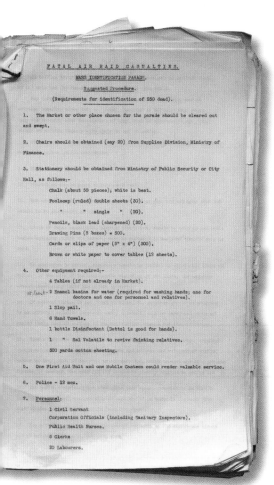

I found a Mrs Lindsay, a St John member, and she and I went round with another group. There was a certain amount of organization. The men's coffins were together and the women's and children's at the other side of the haul (sic). As each was identified it was our duty to put the name of the body and the identifier on the coffin and men moved it to the side where they were put till the relatives removed them for burial. Particulars were handed to the man at the desk. On some of the coffins rough notes were written in chalk. The name of the street where the body had been found, a rude description, 'middle-aged woman, grey hair', 'young girl dark hair', 'fair girl wearing necklace'. We were grateful for these meagre notes for it sometimes saved me exposing the body, by acting as a slight guide towards the identification.

All the way to the place I had told myself I was bound to see horrible sights but only when seen could the full horror be realized. I had seen many dead but they had died in hospital beds, their eyes had been reverently closed, their hands crossed on their breasts; death had, to a certain extent, been glossed over, made decent. It was solemn, tragic, dignified. Here it was grotesque, repulsive, horrible. No attendant nurse had soothed the last moments of these victims, no gentle hands had closed those eyes nor crossed those arms. With tangled hair, staring eyes, clutching hands, contorted limbs, their grey green faces covered with dust they lay, bundled into the coffins, half shrouded in rugs or blankets or an occasional sheet, still wearing their dirty, torn, twisted garments. Death should be dignified, peaceful. Hitler had made even death grotesque.

above/top left
Official Ministry of Public Security file, listing 'Dead identified at St George's Market'
PRONI MPS/2/3/99

left
St George's Market, where Emma worked for a harrowing day, was used as a morgue where bodies were laid out for grieving families to identify them.
© Crown NIEA

I felt outraged. I should have felt pity, sympathy, grief, but instead feelings of repulsion and disgust assailed me. The men who were moving the coffins by means of dirty strips of calico sloped beneath them were of the roughest, coarsest type. One was disfigured by a skin disease. They shouted to each other as they worked. God knows, it was a distasteful enough job and they had been at it for 5 days, enough to stifle finer feelings in more sensitive people. A youngish girl stood in a group dressed in a Red X uniform. She was chewing sweets. 'We've been in since 9.30 this morning. It's an awful job. We're just about fed up', she said, in a common voice. I was sorry for her but shuddered to think of grieving relatives searching amongst those gruesome remains for

82

someone they loved, being accompanied by a girl of that type. It was no job for a girl and nobody should have been kept on it for more than a few hours at a time.

Miss Lindsay and I found to our horror a child of about 7 or 8 sitting on a chair waiting for her mother. How anyone could have allowed a child to enter that Hall of Death I do not know. Mercifully, someone had sat her behind a screen but she could not but have seen those coffins when she entered and she must have known the terrible errand that had brought her mother there. What impression would she carry through life of that day? We got her some tea, a bun and biscuits from the Salvation Army canteen and left her there, though the thought of anybody eating in that place filled me with nausea.

One group of people, consisting of six relatives, seemed to be touring the lines of coffins over and over again, One of the girls, of a very low-looking type, had lost a brother and was looking for another relative. Beside her a strange, rather repulsive creature like a Belcher drawing shuffled, her shabby hat perched on the very top of her head, her twisted hands clasped in front of her.[104] She mumbled and murmured words I could not catch, retailing horrors and I could not help feeling, perhaps unjustly, enjoying a certain amount of satisfaction from being included in the drama and tragedy. One woman was looking in vain for her mother and sister. She had been up from the country on this awful quest 3 days running. She was wrapped in a shawl and her husband looked a rough type but her brother, who had just arrived from Dublin, hoping to carry his brother and sister off to safety and had instead been brought here to seek for their brother, was very well dressed in a good pilot overcoat and soft hat. He was in a terrible state, his face working and twisted, his hands trembling. I wanted to get him a hot drink but found the mobile canteen gone. I asked a policeman where there was a restaurant but he said they were closed round there as they'd run out of food after the Blitz. My two hours' duty drew to an end. The place was closing down till the next day, Sunday. After that any unclaimed bodies were to be buried in a common grave.

I came away drawing deep breaths of fresh air. So this was the result of a Blitz. I had heard of it, pictured it, now seen it. I prayed I would never see it again. I saw in my mind's eye the grey green faces of children, one in

---

[104] George Belcher (1874–1947) was a regular contributor of cartoons to *Punch*.

a coffin with its mother, and the bare foot of a little child, and I heard the voice of a woman in my ear asking for a child, a little boy, 'in velvet trousers'. I tried not to think of it and to think of 'whatsoever things are good, whatsoever things are lovely, whatsoever things are of good report'.[105] Birds, flowers, beautiful skies and seas. Hitler could not distort these.

On Sunday May 4th we had a second 'Blitz'. I do not know how the others reacted but having seen those pathetic streets smashed to dust, those distorted bodies, the horror was brought home to me more but I'm glad to say, though I felt horrified, I did not feel fear. None of the V.A.D.s nor maids showed signs of panic though I sensed a slight shudder as bomb after bomb dropped. The barrage this time was terrific. We soon realized it was an even worse 'Blitz' than the last.[106] As before the up-patients from the women's hospital came down and were accommodated on mattresses on the floor. I had two sick V.A.D.s who were not in hospital because there were not beds for them. One had a badly poisoned thumb and had been given prontosil which made her sick.[107] I managed to get a stretcher for her. Matron was once more ensconced in the passage outside the kitchen. With her tin helmet and gas mask at the alert, a cloak on her shoulders and her very solid legs and her large feet in galoshes, she reminded me of those figures carved out of a single block of wood by peasants. She held an enormous very bright flashlight which at intervals she directed straight on to the faces of the up-patients greatly, I could see, to their resentment.

The thuds of the bombs continued at very short intervals. I thought of Summer Hill and the Riddel Hall where Ruth was, and of Edmund, an A.R.P. warden at Craigavad and Celia, nervous but brave, the only woman at the A.R.P. centre above their house at Holywood. Occasionally

[105] Philippians 4:8: 'Finally, brethren, whatsoever things are true, whatsoever things are honest, whatsoever things are just, whatsoever things are pure, whatsoever things are lovely, whatsoever things are of good report; if there be any virtue, and if there be any praise, think on these things.'

[106] The noise of the bombing may well have been worse than was the case on the Easter Tuesday raid but this may have been because the bombs landed closer to their original targets, the docks area, and closer to Stranmillis. And the casualty rate was greatly reduced, the number of fatalities being 199. However, it was the fires that created most impression. 'At peak there were over 200 fires burning' from the 3,500 incendiaries dropped. (Barton, op. cit. pp 369–372)

[107] Prontosil was a pre-penicillin antibiotic developed in the mid-1930s by German pharmaceutical scientists from its original form, a red industrial dye.

84

I went up the stairs into the hall to see the V.A.D. patients on stretchers there. The great hall door shuddered and shook in the blast but stood fast. One of the orderlies asked me if I would like to go and look out of the window where the fire watchers were. He led me along a dark passage. I looked with something like despair at the town. The sky was red above it, great clouds of smoke were eddying and billowing from the direction of the lough. I thought of the people who had already endured the last blitz, crawling in terror in the shelters in the already shattered areas.

About 4 o'clock it ended and we came back to the quarters. The smell of burning was in the air. The grass was strewn with blackened and charred papers. There was a sheet from some child's essay book. On the top of the page I read 'The end of the world'. It seemed appropriate. It was the end of the world as we knew it; let us hope it will be the beginning of a better one.

Hospital work had to go on in spite of blitzes and some casualties had been brought in. The maids were wonderful. Somehow breakfast was got on the table at 7 as usual. I arranged for the maids to go off in relays and rest as much as possible. I went to Donegall Rd hospital, calling at Summer Hill and Riddel Hall to find all well, except both the maids had fled. While I was at Donegall Rd hospital the sirens went and we put on our steel helmets and put our gas masks at the alert. Little Miss Shine who had been nervous at the last raid was in bed after an inoculation for T.A.B. but she said she'd got accustomed to it now, she hadn't been nearly so scared.[108] She'd been on leave and travelled with evacuees to Dublin. One woman, she said, had a dead baby in her arms and was asking for a bottle for it from anyone she met. Eire had opened her arms to the refugees and the Dublin and Dundalk fire brigades had arrived after the blitzes, cheered by the crowds.[109] Perhaps this will draw north and south closer. I wonder!

Claim made for air raid damage to the gardener's hut at Riddel Hall, Stranmillis Road, where Emma's sister, Ruth was principal 1913-43.

PRONI D3119/2/12

[109] Eamon de Valera, Taoiseach, had permitted tenders from southern fire stations to cross the border. 'In total', says Barton *op. cit.*, p. 239, 'seventy men and thirteen fire engines were … dispatched from Dublin, Dundalk, Drogheda and Dun Laoghaire'.

The oldest part of the city centre, looking down Bridge Street from High Street. The Northern Whig building is still standing but Arnott's department store, on the corner, has been destroyed.

Belfast Telegraph

This time tremendous damage had been done, but more in the shopping centre and though it looked much worse there were not so many lives lost. I had left a uniform coat and shirt in at a tailor's to be pressed and a tweed skirt. I peered down the street but could see only smouldering rubble. Molly unfortunately the day before had left her watch and a little clock at the watchmaker's. It too was gone. How we would have fussed over these things in peace time. Now we took it in our stride.

Another of the V.A.D.s had lost her home. Her brother, an A.R.P. warden, had arrived the morning after the blitz and asked to speak to her but wanted me to tell her first none of her people was hurt. One of the two night sisters had just given her report to Matron and I thought I would get in before the other began as the man looked dead and I did not want to keep him. 'Matron', I began after knocking at her door, 'May I send for Miss Gilmore. She's lost her home?'. She waved me outside. 'I'll see you in a few seconds'. 'But Matron', I protested, her brother's here. 'I'll see you in a few seconds', she repeated, not even inquiring if Miss Gilmore's people were killed. I retired, fuming.

'Have you had anything to eat all night?' I asked the brother. He shook his head. 'Mary', I said, 'give this man some breakfast'. He walked in and sat down in the mess. I knew Matron would be furious if she saw him but I didn't care. Sister's report was long but at last Matron sent for me. I told her curtly what I wanted. 'Send Miss Gilmore here', she said, 'ring up and tell sister to send her down'. 'But Matron', I said 'her brother doesn't want to see her till she knows they're all safe'. 'Send her here. I'll break it to her', she said coldly. 'I'll go across and tell her', I said equally firmly. 'Oh, all right, if you like to tell her', she said, with no good grace. I went and told her and brought her

PRONI D3119/2/4

A notice issued by the Belfast Civil Defence Authority advising what to do about 'missing friends and relatives' in the aftermath of a raid.

facing page
An iconic view of the devastation wrought by the air raids. In spite of all, the Albert Clock, at the foot of High Street, remains defiantly upright.
PRONI CAB/3/A/68

down to speak to her brother. She was wonderfully calm and said she'd go over at her off duty time to see what she could save.

It was not the only bad news I had to break. Miss Love, my nice little lady cook, got a wire to say her brother was seriously ill. She walked in to the station to find what train she could catch to Derry in the morning and while away the police rang from Derry to say he was dead. It was late and I decided not to tell her till the morning. When she got back from the station I sent her to bed with a hot drink and vegamine[110] and was then called to Betty the maid who had just heard her sister had been found in the ruins of a house where she was the maid, the only one taken out alive and she was in the Mater hospital with an injured head, broken arms and injuries to leg. Poor Betty was in floods of tears. I comforted her as well as I could, got her a hot drink and vegamine and got her into bed and went to bed myself, feeling very tired. I hadn't got to bed long before the sirens went and we all had to go to Stranmillis House.

I felt terribly sorry for Betty who after what she had heard of her sister must have felt shattered. All night I thought of Miss Love and how I would have to break the news of her brother's death to her before she left in the morning. We got back to bed at about 4 am when the all clear went. I would have loved a long lie but knew it was out of the question. The maids were wonderful for they got 7 o'clock breakfast ready. I sent Miss Love hers in bed and when she'd had it I braced myself to go and tell her. Poor little girl, she clung to me like a child, sobbing on my shoulder, but she was good and pulled herself together. I got her a taxi and sent Miss Connor, the other lady cook, to the station with her. The next night we had the sirens again. Everyone was getting very weary but carried on. Another of my V.A.D.s went sick and two of the maids got wires from their people to go home. One of the V.A.D. cooks from the hospital came in to the House to cook for the V.A.D.s and we managed somehow. My leave was a month overdue and I had intended to go to Rostrevor with Celia and Harry but I couldn't put in for it under the circumstances. I saw them depart with a pang for I longed for a peaceful time in the country, away not only from the blitzes but from the continual minor worries.

All the new V.A.D.s were to have T.A.B. injections, all the more important now since the blitz. To get Matron to consent to spare them off the wards

---

[110] Dilutable food enhancer used in soups, hot drinks, etc.

88

Smouldering buildings alongside St Anne's Cathedral, Lower Donegall Street, which had been completed shortly before the war started.

PRONI CAB/3/A/68

Premier's Message to Ulster *April 19.*

THE Prime Minister, Mr. J. M. Andrews, issued the following statement yesterday :—

" The people of Belfast have been subjected to a cruel and inhuman ordeal by an enemy who has carried barbarity to its utmost limits. I have seen the devastation in the bombed areas of the city, and have observed with unstinted admiration the quiet heroism and splendid fortitude of our people. Their trial is severe and tragic beyond words to express, but they are bearing it with a spirit that is unbreakable.

" Now that the first shock of this foul attack is past, we must all turn our attention to the problem of restoring, as far as possible, the normal life of the community. I earnestly appeal to all sections of the population to work together wholeheartedly and courageously to achieve this.

" Our civil defence services and voluntary workers are striving, with unceasing devotion, to alleviate the distress and suffering amongst the civil population. But there is still much to be done, and each one of us, I know, will ask himself ' What more can I do to help ? ' Employers and work-people can render a great public service by showing mutual help-fulness and making a strenuous effort to increase output. House-holders can manifest good-neigh-bourliness and eagerness to help their fellows. The authorities have a gigantic task before them, and it is the privilege of everyone to co-operate with them by obeying instructions implicitly, responding willingly to all appeals, and dis-playing throughout this emergency the highest qualities of citizenship.

" I do not forget the people of the areas outside Belfast who have been affected by the raid. To them, as well as to the citizens of Belfast, my message is sent.

" We all suffer with one another. We are one in heart and purpose—united against a brutal foe. We will see this thing through to the end, so that we may rejoice together in the day of victory."

" CARRY ON "
Lord Mayor's Call to Citizens

"AS Lord Mayor I wish, on behalf of the citizens of Belfast, to offer sincere sympathy to those who have been bereaved, to those who have been injured, and also to those who have suffered severe loss by the recent enemy attack on our city," said Sir Crawford M'Cullagh, Bart., in a message issued yesterday.

" May I say how proud we are of the high courage shown by everyone, and the magnificent way they have stood up to this dastardly attack?

" The services rendered by the personnel of the Civil Defence in dealing with the difficult situation and aiding the victims is very highly appreciated.

" It remains now for each of us to carry on to the best of his or her ability, to support the authorities, and to render every assistance possible to each other."

PRONI CAB/3/A/68

or to arrange beforehand entailed a continued struggle. According to King's Regulations they were entitled to 48 hours (for 1st T.A.B.) off duty, but she grudged them being off at all. Many had not yet had their medical exams because the doctor was too busy. Added to this all the V.A.D.s were to attend gas lectures and they had to be chosen daily. It involved endless discussion, grumbles from Matron, and demonstrations of bad temper, grunts from the sisters who had to spare them, groans from the V.A.D.s who had to attend on off duty time. I had to listen to them all and try and smooth the path and often felt exhausted, trying to please everyone.

Parties of soldiers aided civilians to clear up Belfast. Large gaps appeared where flourishing shops had stood. Spaces were roped off because of delayed-action bombs. People had to leave their homes at 10 minutes' notice. One bomb was discovered in a football ground 6 days after the blitz and everyone round was told to evacuate. Experts were brought from England to examine it but failed to recognise its species!

5 AFTERMATH, CHANGES AND DEMOBILISATION

The period following the dramatic Luftwaffe air raids on Belfast amounted to something of an anti-climax for Emma. On resuming her 'normal' duties as VAD Commandant she found herself in renewed and personally disquieting conflict with the Matron of the military hospital, all of which she found unseemly and perplexing. It came to a head on the question of organising a nurses' dance, as a result of which Emma concluded she had not been shown the respect both she personally and her position as Commandant deserved. Some indication of the toll this disagreeable episode took on Emma can be seen in the almost abrupt ending of the diary entries from (as far as can be established) some time late in 1942 or early 1943.

Some thirty-five years later, in 1967, Emma rounds off the story of her involvement until she was demobbed . This postscript is interesting because it raises an issue, of how she handled the pregnancy of one of the nurses in her charge, that she may not have felt at liberty to mention a generation earlier. In fact she comments that 'the reason I record this sad event is ... to emphasise the contrast in the attitude towards 'sex' during the wars.'

Over thirty years later Emma's postscript makes clear the extent to which she was, understandably, disenchanted by the changes in the VAD regulations brought about by the introduction in 1943 of the recommendations of the Elliott Report. Not only did this see the nurses lose their 'volunteer' status and be incorporated into the army system as privates but, just as dismayingly for Emma, the rank of Commandant was abolished, leaving her in an anomalous position. Emma was offered another army rank which she 'curtly refused'. Typically, she stayed on until her long overdue demobilisation papers came through, by which time she could record with equal measures of dignity and disappointment that she was 'sorry that my career with the army after two wars should end so unsatisfactorily'.

diary pages 112–138

After a quiet spell I put in for leave and Dorothy and I went to Rostrevor. The hotel was full, officers and their wives and bombed out people. The latter were marvellous. They spoke of it so calmly as if their experiences were nothing unusual and were most philosophical over their losses. A Mrs Shannon, a bank manager's wife, who was very lame, had been bombed out the night of the first raid and had taken refuge in another bank opposite from theirs. From there she had proceeded to the Mater hospital and while there the nurses' home was hit. Such of her belongings that were saved she had got one of the big furniture shops to store. This had been bombed in the 2nd raid and completely demolished, so she had lost everything. Her chief regret was for a beautiful old bureau which had contained, amongst other things, a lot of family miniatures. She was however still bright and cheery. Another lady from Bangor described sitting under the stairs in the first raid while her house crumbled above them.[111]

The hotel was exceedingly comfortable, the food good and except for a rationing of butter everything appeared as in peace time. The weather was lovely. Our only complaint was it was too hot. Dorothy and I spent a good deal of time in the hotel garden, overlooking Carlingford Lough towards the mountains of 'neutral' Eire. We took occasional bus drives and picnicked out and went out to tea once with a Miss O'Loughlin who I discovered I had been at school with.[112] She had let her house, which was in a lovely situation on the lough side and was living in a converted stable in the old walled-in garden on the other side of the wood.

The week flew past and before I knew I was back again. Matron had chosen Sister Hallett to do my job while I was on leave. Sister Hallett had only just arrived from England and did not know one of the V.A.D.s by name even. Added to that she had not been given time for me to show her the ropes or hand over to her properly. Consequently, through no fault of hers I found things in a hopeless muddle. Matron had elected to do some of the work herself and amongst other things had handed in

---

[111] Barton *op. cit.*, p. 315, 'Fourteen bombs are reported to have fallen on Bangor' during the April raid, killing five people.

[112] Florence Marie O'Loughlin was one of three daughters of Revd Dr R. S. O'Loughlin, rector, Lurgan Parish Church, who attended Cheltenham Ladies' College in the early 1900s, at the same time as Emma. Florence returned as a teacher before taking up a position at Somerville College, Oxford, where she died as Lady Woodward in 1961. (My thanks to Rachel Roberts, Archivist, Cheltenham Ladies' College, for this information.)

notes re V.A.D.s to be put on Part II orders, which were quite incorrect and I had to have them altered and contradicted or their pay would have gone wrong. These Part II orders were always a bit of a nightmare. We published them weekly and anything concerning VADs, their leave, sickness, washing allowance etc etc had to appear, with any promotions or upgrading and these were supposed to be copied by 15 Coy. Part II orders published at Holywood. The paymaster in England did not see our orders. He only saw 15 Coy. orders and if they omitted anything, which they constantly did, the V.A.D.s' pay was immediately affected. If, for instance, a V.A.D. had been upgraded and received her pay at the higher grade rate but the date of the upgrading had been omitted or put in under the wrong date, a curt note would reach us from the paymaster to say that the V.A.D. was in debt and that we must immediately reduce her pay till her debt was wiped out. Owing to the fact that the paymaster's staff was no doubt overwhelmed with work they were never up to date and the debt to be re-claimed might date back to months or even years back.

One would have thought it would have simplified matters considerably if the paymaster had condescended to say why the girl was in debt. As it was it involved endless research through back numbers of the Stranmillis and Holywood orders, first to find the 'slip up' and after that Holywood had to be persuaded to rectify it. One V.A.D. for instance had joined in 1939 as an Immobile member. Immobile members drew a lower rate of pay than Mobile ones. Then she had been told Immobile members were not required so she had become Mobile and was paid at mobile rate but Holywood had omitted to show the change-over in Part II orders. In 1941 the paymaster realised that an Immobile member had been paid at mobile rates since 1939 and showed her in debt for the whole amount and notified us to restrict her pay but gave no reason. After a day or two's concentration, I discovered the mistake with a sense of triumph. I had won the first round of the game. But it took endless correspondence and telephone calls to convince Holywood that I was right and it was not till I got a confirmation from the paymaster that my conclusion was correct that Holywood rectified the mistake by putting her in order as 'Mobile' (w.e.f.1939) I having got the date off the duplicate 'Mobile' form which fortunately she was able to produce.

Then another four were shown in debt, greatly to their indignation. After much research and endless correspondence over weeks during which time their pay was restricted causing very natural dissatisfaction, it was traced back to an incorrect order published by Holywood in 1939. The coy office there had discovered that the date was wrong and corrected the order but had failed to publish the correct date, with dire consequences. This correspondence actually went to Headquarters North Ireland district before the mistake was amended.

Then there was the case of the cooks. The cooks, when they joined, had all been graded as hospital cooks grade 1 and paid accordingly and some had been promoted sergeants and corporals on the strength of training in civilian cookery schools of former experience. My sergeant Cook, Miss Wilson, had spent three years at Atholl Crescent in Edinburgh and was a first-class cook.[113] Suddenly the paymaster discovered that none of them had the certificates mentioned in R.A.M.C. standing orders therefore none of them were entitled to be Grade 1 cooks. Accordingly he issued orders to the various units (all of which including the English ones had likewise graded their V.A.D.s G[rade] 1) that they were to publish an order de-grading the cooks to Grade III. No sooner did these orders appear than the units were notified that all their cooks were in debt and their pay was immediately restricted. Then began the battle of the cooks which, as I write, has lasted exactly one year and is now drawing to a triumphant conclusion, a win for us but at what a sacrifice of time, paper, stamps, not to mention wear and tear on nerves and temper. I spent days and weeks over this battle, feeling again and again as if I were striking my head against a stone wall and falling back exhausted but rallying myself for another struggle. This sounds an exaggeration but it is literally true. If the V.A.D. cooks had not been sweet-tempered and patient, and fortunately the majority not dependent on their earnings, the disagreeables and difficulties would have been even greater. Harry Randall was also a great support. He brought a nice col. and major from the W.O. to tea with me to whom I could pour out all my woes and they advised me who to write to and how to tackle the problem.

Eventually a letter came from the W.O. to say that an A.C.I. (Army Council Instruction) would shortly be published dealing with the matter. We had to sit back and wait for months for the A.C.I. Harry duly informed me when it appeared, long before it drifted into the coy office. This laid down that

[113] The Edinburgh Cookery School at Atholl Crescent, Edinburgh had been established in the 1870s.

the cooks were to have a test by the catering officer and if passed as proficient could be re-graded and on his recommendation that it should be made retrospective. Applications could be made to the G.O.C. and if he sanctioned it they could appear in order as G.1 from date of joining which was most important as the money that had been taken off them would now be credited to them again.

After another few weeks the catering officer made an appointment to grade the cooks including the two from Donegall Rd. Now it was laid down in the V.A.D.s' war regulations that no V.A.D. of less than 1st class grade could hold the rank of N.C.O. This should have automatically reduced my sergeant and corporals to the ranks but nobody but myself had tumbled to this anomaly and they had continued to draw N.C.O.s' pay and consequently had never suffered financially but I strongly recommended them to take the test in case this mistake was discovered. The cooks' battle ended a year and 3 months after I first started the struggle and 10 months after the W.O. letter authorizing the re-grading and re-payment of debt was published. So much for army methods. Any business firm would have been bankrupt in a month and their employees would have walked out and sued them for arrears of pay.

Meanwhile Col. Booth was superannuated and replaced by Col. Grant. I was sorry to see him go. He had always been a good friend to me but he was not a 'live wire' and was rather on Chamberlain's lines of 'peace at any price'. He patted me on the shoulder and said I had been a great help to him. Alas! Matron did not depart with him. She had been growing more and more impossible and I had gone to him once, unwillingly, and told him I couldn't stand it much longer. Mr Warren, the Q.M., rather a cocky, chubby little fellow, wishing to show a good budget, had got the C.O. in an unwary moment to sign an order that lights must be out in V.A.D. quarters at 10 pm. I thought it too early but as Col. Booth had signed the order I obeyed it and turned off lights every night. Matron, who trusted nobody, used to come down to see that lights were out. This annoyed me very much and one night when I had unwittingly left them 10 minutes beyond the time I was furious to hear them being switched off in the corridor and my own lights went off also. I groped my way out wrathfully to find Matron in a towering rage asking why lights were not out. The next day I went to the C.O. and said if I could not be trusted to turn off lights I would send in my resignation but I would not stand the way I was being treated. He begged me not to resign and said he would speak to the Principal Matron about the way Miss McC[114] was behaving as she was making everyone miserable. Whether he did or not I never knew but for a bit she was better to me and she never came down about the lights again but alas she did not leave for many months afterwards.

Col. Grant was better able to cope with her and stuck up mostly for me and the V.A.D.s. I found him very easy and pleasant and quite enjoyed my morning interviews with him which were not always strictly confined to business. He was keen on painting and we used to discuss painters and he showed me his drawings. I used to think how angry Matron would be could she have looked through the wall and seen us or hear him describing her as 'the baby piano' or referring to her as 'Ma'. Not very loyal, perhaps, but she did not earn and did not receive loyalty or respect from anyone. I have never met anyone so lacking in courtesy or consideration.

The Donegall Rd hospital had been closed down after the Blitz as it was in rather a congested area and it was moved to the country, to Benburb, an adapted house outside Armagh. There was no accommodation for V.A.D.s there so they were sent to us and as the V.A.D. quarters were full they had to be accommodated in the sisters' bungalow, greatly to Matron's annoyance. She refused to allow them to come in and out by the sisters' entrance and they had to cross a grass plot and come in by the cloakroom door. All very well in fine weather but we had a particularly wet summer and soon the track across the plot was a slime slide and later a bog. I went to the Q.M. but he said nothing could be done as it was not an official path. Eventually, after appealing to the colonel the engineers made an official path, I've no doubt at great expense to avoid Matron having to have the sisters' quarters polluted by V.A.D.s. I wonder what she'd have thought in the last war where V.A.D.s messed and often had to share rooms with sisters in France.

It was a very wet summer. The war news was not very cheering and the thought of winter not encouraging. I asked Matron if I could have my leave in September as my family were going to Newcastle but she

---

[114] The matron's name is fully spelled out here but as Emma had previously referred to her as 'Miss McC' and had indeed scribbled out her full name, this convention has been continued.

immediately said she wanted to go on leave herself then I was so pleased to think of being without her for a week it was as good [as] a second week to me. Then we were told that the D.M.S. (Director of Medical Services) was coming from London to inspect the hospital and my leave was again postponed. The day before he came and that morning everyone was doing something, cleaning, polishing. I was told he might inspect the quarters so we were hard at work making everything spick and span. We heard he'd arrived in hospital and presently I saw Matron ponderously ascending the hill alone. I gathered the main hospital had been inspected and there would be a pause before he proceeded to 'officers', the house on the top of the hill. I thought I'd find out from Matron if he were coming through the quarters. I met her outside her door and asked her. 'Not yours', she said rudely, and slammed the door in my face. I had to laugh. It was so obvious that she was determined I should not meet the general who, incidentally, was a Belfast man though I did not know him. I went back to my room and presently an orderly appeared to say he'd been sent by the C.O. to tell me to go up to 'officers' and be introduced to the general. One in the eye for Matron, I thought, chuckling, as I powdered my nose and pulled on my hat. When I reached officers the hall seemed full of people. The C.O., the coy officers, the Q.M., the sgt-major, the general, the A.D.M.S., aide-de-camp etc etc. I was introduced to the general who asked me was I Adam Duffin's daughter as he had known him well.[115] McC. stood by with a very false smile while he chatted to me. What a mind! This was before Col. Booth left. Personally, I didn't care whether I met the general or not but I thought it nice of the colonel to send for me.

Another winter started and the misery of the 'black out' began again. Bad as it was in private houses it was worse in quarters. There were 50 bedrooms, each with a window in my bungalow not to mention sitting rooms and kitchen and my own rooms, and to see that there were no lights showing was almost a one man's (sic) job. Unfortunately for me, my bungalow was the first and any light showing was visible for miles. Miss McC always took it for granted that if a light was shining it must be the V.A.D.s' fault, though actually they were always much better about lights than the sisters but their bungalow was more hidden and they were seldom betrayed. Many a time I was rung up on the telephone by Matron

[115] Emma's father, Adam Duffin, a well-doing businessman and sometime President of the Belfast Chamber of Commerce and a prominent Unionist politician, had died in 1924.

to say a light was shining and I would stumble around in the dark and often in the rain and fail to find it. Later she would ask me furiously which girl was responsible and when I answered truthfully that I hadn't been able to trace it, she looked sceptical and obviously believed that I was concealing the culprit's name though actually I was very severe if I did catch anyone being careless. Another thing that made her furious was anyone ringing up a V.A.D. on the telephone which unfortunately was outside her room and she insisted on having it switched through to her, though other matrons wisely ordered it to be [put] through to our end so that we could switch it through to her if she required it.

Towards Christmas the V.A.D.s approached me and said they would like to give a dance in the V.A.D.s' dining room. The year before Miss Irwin, the Holywood V.A.D. commandant had expressed surprise that we had danced there as she had been warden at Stranmillis when it had been a training college and had expressed surprise at our dancing there [and] had reported the floor had not been considered safe for dancing. Accordingly I warned the V.A.D.s that they would not be able to hold it there but I would ask Matron. The minute I mentioned it she said 'They can't dance in the quarters. The floor's not safe'. I accepted this and the V.A.D.s agreed to go ahead with the dance though it would cost a good deal more as not only could they not get the supper cooked and served by the staff but they would also have to pay for a hall. They arranged for a hall and to pay so much a head for their guests which included supper. They asked me to take so much a week from each girl till a sum to pay for the dance had accumulated and I gave them a subscription. The reason for these details being recorded is because of what subsequently occurred.

They had a mess meeting and decided that each girl could ask two guests but would have to pay for them. In addition, out of the mess money a certain number from the sgts' and orderlies' mess were to be invited. Also the colonel and the medical officers and their wives. One of the Donegall Rd V.A.D.s raised the question were they to ask the 'sisters' as they did not ask V.A.D.s to their dances. I said it was their dance and they must decide themselves but they must remember officers went to N.C.O.s' and privates' messes for dances though they did not ask them back. Later they told me they certainly would like to ask the sisters, greatly to my relief though as I did not want to coerce them. I thought it would make bad feeling if they were not asked. They very generously asked Matron and 13 sisters. The mess committee asked me to receive the guests with them and we

Emma's illustrations included Christmas cards, shown here. The 'CR' at the end of the verses indicates they were written by Emma's married sister, Celia Randall.

E.S.Duffin

My bell rings out the children throng, To hear me call: O yes! O yes! Christmas is here with dance & song To fill the day with happiness! In children's hands the Christmas rose, The berried fruits that winter brings, Are gifts of love as great as those Were brought to Bethlehem by kings.

And as I ring the years recede, And once again old memories start Along those magic lines that lead From place to place, from heart to heart, O yes, O yes! Across the snow, My bell rings out to sea and hill. Love that was born so long ago Is here today & changeless still.

C.R.

ordered two taxis to go up early with us. They also asked me if I would do six dance programmes to go round the hall. I did them with little figures of sisters, M.O.s, V.A.D.s etc dancing and they were very pleased with them.

The morning of the dance Matron said 'How are you going to the dance?'. I said Major Harris, the coy officer had arranged for a bus for the V.A.D.s and I and the messing committee were going up early in two taxis. 'I'll come in your taxi', she said. I couldn't very well refuse. Accordingly she came but I was hardly prepared for what happened. She received all the guests and introduced them to me and even gave me orders how to manage the supper. The V.A.D.s were furious. She then looked at my programme and said 'I would like one of these. Keep one for me'. Again the V.A.D.s were furious. They had decided to draw lots for them as souvenirs and I had stipulated one should be kept for Miss Ellison, a V.A.D. who had just had her appendix out and could not come.

The dance went well. The A.D.M.S. and his wife came and the col. and his wife. Major Harris conducted the band and arranged spot light dances etc. The V.A.D.s looked after their guests well. The sisters were gracious and said it was the best dance they had been at. Matron offered two naval officers lifts in our taxi so the messing committee went back in the bus! Later Matron told me the sisters wanted to give a dance too and asked me what the V.A.D.s had paid for the hall and how much per head for the supper, in case they wanted to give it in the same place.

I heard no more till one day till some of the V.A.D.s came to me and asked me if it were true that the sisters were going to give a dance in the V.A.D.s' dining room. I said of course not; they knew the floor wasn't considered safe. Also I had heard nothing of it and as a member of the sisters' mess of course I would have. Also, Matron would have asked me about using the V.A.D.s' dining room. I little knew! The rumours persisted and it was Mary, the sisters' head maid, who told me it was settled. Matron had got the engineers to test the floor. Even the date was settled and Miss Conor, the sisters' little lady cook, had been told she was to arrange the supper. My feelings are better imagined than described. If Matron wished, she could have got the engineers to test the floor for the V.A.D.s and saved them pounds of money. I asked Miss Conor if it were true. Yes, matron had spoken to her. She was worried and distressed. How could she provide a dance supper? Rations were so much tighter than they were last year, at the time of the other dance. Also, Miss McGeary was there to help organise and a friend of their own, an experienced cook, had come in to help. Miss Love, the V.A.D.s' cook said of course she would help Miss Conor, though Matron had never mentioned it to her.

I went to Matron's office and said 'Matron, is it true the sisters are giving a dance in the V.A.D.s' dining room?' 'Who told you?', she said rudely. 'Nothing is settled yet' but I knew this was untrue as I had heard she'd called a mess committee and it had been settled. Also I had Miss Conor and Mary's evidence. 'I've had the floor tested by the engineers. It's perfectly safe', she added. 'Who told you about it?' she continued. 'I heard it from Mary' I said grimly. 'You shouldn't listen to tales from maids', she said insolently'. 'And I shouldn't hear it from maids. I should have heard it at the messing committee to which I was not invited'. She looked slightly taken aback. 'The meeting was called in a hurry on Sunday evening', she said, 'and you are always out on a Sunday evening'. A lame excuse. Nothing more was said.

The preparations for the dance continued. From Mary again I learned the date was fixed. I could no longer conceal the fact from my V.A.D.s. I spoke to Matron again, I told her I had always wished for a good atmosphere between sisters and V.A.D.s but this would ruin it. 'We intend to ask 3 V.A.D.s', she said. This was the last straw. If sisters were officers and couldn't have V.A.D.s in their mess I would accept that but if they could be asked, to ask 3 to a dance in their dining room, to a supper partly cooked by their own cook when they had paid so much a head to entertain Matron and 13 sisters. 'If they only intend to ask 3', I said, 'it would be much better not to ask any'. 'It isn't settled yet how many will be asked', she said.

When I went in to see the colonel about something, he told me Matron had told him the whole story. 'Of course', he said, trying to pour oil on the troubled waters,' you know the V.A.D.s gave their dance before the floor was tested by the engineers'. 'Yes', I said bitterly, 'nobody thought of having it tested for them and they had to pay a lot for the dance they gave'. And he went on 'You know officers do go to other ranks' dances but don't ask them back'. 'Yes', I said, 'but you don't borrow their mess room without even the courtesy of asking, to give your dances'. 'No', he said, 'of course, they intend to ask you and some of the V.A.D.s'. 'Ask me!', I said, 'I'm a member of the sisters' mess, and 3 V.A.D.s were mentioned and I've advised Matron it would be much better not to ask any'. He reluctantly agreed for like all men he didn't want to be drawn into a disagreement and I don't blame him. I would not have mentioned it to him had not Matron already done so.

No more was said. I spoke to Sister Baker, one of the senior sisters, and told her what I thought of the situation and she was distressed. She thought the V.A.D.s had chosen to give their dance outside out of preference. She had never imagined that Matron had not asked me about the dining room. She agreed the situation was impossible but said the invitations had gone out. Nothing could be done. I explained I did not want them to think the V.A.D.s were grudging about lending the sisters their dining room; it was the way the thing had been done. She fully agreed and no doubt passed it on to the other sisters. Nobody mentioned the dance in my presence.

When I went to pay Matron my messing money she said 'Will you let me have the names of the guests you want to ask to the dance before midday'.

Mary the maid was in the room so I said nothing. 'I will let you know later', intending to see her but it was Inspection morning, so I didn't. Accordingly, I wrote a note and left it on her desk in which I said 'I feel very strongly about this dance. I have no intention of asking any guests to it nor do I intend to be at it. With your permission I shall take a day off and go home that night. I don't know if you intend to invite the V.A.D.s. In their place I would not accept but I shall not influence them one way or the other. If they refuse I shall not urge them to go'.

I did not see Matron till the next day; she made no reference to my note. The V.A.D.s were not asked. In the morning of the dance Matron said to me, 'You want to take a day off today, don't you, Miss Duffin?' I said 'Yes'. Nobody referred to the dance again in my presence. I told the V.A.D.s the action I had taken. They were furious about it. The incident was then closed but I and the V.A.D.s disliked Matron more than ever.

1967

I ceased to keep this diary. I don't now remember why. I suppose I was too busy and once having made the break I did not begin again but now, after nearly 30 years, there are some events I feel I should record but I record them from memory, not when they happened.

Matron was posted to Benburb, of all places, Rather a come down for her! Everyone was delighted. As I made my way down the drive to the hospital, I met a V.A.D. 'Matron's posted', she said, with a beaming smile. Then an orderly. 'Matron's posted' said he with a grin. Sad to be so unloved, perhaps, but she deserved it.

Her place was taken by a charming, much younger woman, efficient and pleasant to look on. She had been a V.A.D. herself in World War 1 and was sympathetic towards V.A.D.s which made my task easier. Alas, she didn't stay very long. The Matron-in-Chief evidently believed in keeping staff on the move. I served under 7 or 8 Matrons. They generally left at a day's notice and the one who took over began from scratch, making many changes. This did not lead to good management and was very bad for the hospital and what purpose it served I cannot imagine.

There were notices for civilians posted up everywhere 'is your journey really necessary?' yet sisters from Stranmillis [who] received orders to report in London were then sent back to Belfast 'to await instructions'. V.A.D.s, no matter where their homes were, were given passes and free transport to any part of the British Isles for their leave if they so desired. They often went to London, the last place they should have gone. I went to London myself to represent the St John at a meeting. I stayed at my club and was able to see the Misses Anne and Deirdre and spent a night or two at Sevenoaks with the Crum Ewings.[116] I came in for 2 bad raids. There was no 'shelter' attached to the club so we sat in the darkened hall. The morning I was to start off for London I had a shock as one of the V.A.D.s had had a miscarriage. I had known she was expecting a baby and had arranged for her to go home. The dreadful part was that the M.O. who operated said she had brought on the miscarriage and killed the baby by so doing but it was hushed up. She was diagnosed 'discharged on account of permanent bronchitis' which was true. I offered to give up my leave but as I was going on business Matron insisted on my going.

The reason I record this sad event is because it was to emphasise the contrast in the attitude towards 'sex' during the wars. I served in the 1st war in Egypt and France for 4 years and never heard of a V.A.D. in this kind of trouble and I questioned my sisters and other friends who had served in England and France and neither had they, but in this war there were in my small district, 2 hospitals, 4 cases of V.A.D.s having babies. It is not for me to condemn these girls but I think the other outlook was better and healthier though I am aware that many present day people would disagree with me. It certainly caused suffering and led to deception and lying on the mother's part and in most cases children, though cared for, brought up in unnatural surroundings.

IS YOUR JOURNEY REALLY NECESSARY?

TICKETS

RAILWAY EXECUTIVE COMMITTEE

The public was encouraged to bear in mind the importance of fuel rationing in the general war effort.

---

[116] Anne and Deirdre were Emma's nieces, daughters of her brother Terence, who had died in 1936.

At this time the W.O., inspired if not bullied by the Matron-in-Chief, Miss Jones, decided that army sisters were to hold commissions. Hitherto they had only had the honorary rank of 'officers'. Miss Jones felt that it was unfair that army sisters who had served in the army long before any other women's corps had been formed, held no rank. One can sympathise with this attitude up to a point but the 'sisters' were in a unique position and had always enjoyed the respect of all ranks. To me it seemed a terrible mistake for them to compete with captains and colonels and officers in the W.A.A.C., W.R.A.F. etc. However, they duly received their commissions. They did not drill or go on parades and Matrons who had always received a courtesy salute from the orderlies had now to return it by a somewhat self-conscious furtive salute.[117]

As a consequence of the sisters becoming officers, the V.A.D.s were automatically to become privates. They were given the choice of transferring into the services thus depriving the hospitals of their 2 or 3 years experience as nurses. Many of the English V.A.D.s took advantage of this. As there was no conscription in Northern Ireland my V.A.D.s had the right to resign and all my best V.A.D.s did so. I did not try to influence them in any way beyond reminding them that in wartime one had to put up with a lot. I felt very sad about it. The V.A.D.s had given good service through the two wars and were now no longer to be 'nurses' but privates. The admiralty decided to keep their V.A.D.s as they had been, and many of the V.A.D.s might have transferred to this service, but Miss Jones fearing this might happen had had a clause put in regulations preventing this. This seemed to me petty and mean and I was thoroughly disgusted. The Colonel and most of the sisters were as indignant as I was.[118]

Lady Mountbatten came over to talk to me and Miss Irwin, the other V.A.D. commandant, about it. She assured us that she and Lady Limerick representing the Red X (Lady Mt Batten represented St John) had done their best to avert the change but had fought in vain. They had, she

[117] Wide-ranging changes were made to the role and status of VAD nurses, sisters and Matrons by the War Office (1943) *Report of the Committee on Voluntary Aid Detachments, The Elliott Committee*, (Cmd. 6448), (London: HMSO).

[118] Emma was dismayed by the Elliott Report recommendations insofar as they took away the V.A.D. nurses' 'volunteer' status and effectively made them army privates. Her own rank, Commandant, was abolished. Commandants were to be offered the rank of Warrant Officer, which she declined.

pointed out, won some points, the V.A.D.s were still to wear St John and Red X uniform, though they were to be incorporated into the A.T.S. (now the W.R.A.C.). I said bitterly that though this was a concession their uniform allowance and washing allowance did not cover half their expenses while the A.T.S. had even their underclothing provided. Also, they would be the only girls in the services as the commandants were 'scrapped' or transferred to other services. Lady Mountbatten was disappointed that I did not accept the changes but I stuck to my guns. I did not mind losing my job but I minded the V.A.D.s being left.[119] Later I got a letter from the W.O. asking me if I would like to remain with the rank sergeant major! Harry served through two wars with this rank of officer. I curtly refused but alas was not demobbed for some time.[120] The V.A.D.s who resigned were replaced by A.T.S. with no nursing experiences. The sisters complained that sometimes they did not appear and explained they'd been on parade or disobeyed orders and when spoken to said 'I'll speak to my officer', their officers being the A.T.S. officers, not the sisters. It may work smoothly now, I don't know, but I smile when I see a Matron referred to as a Lieut. Colonel.

The recommendations of the Elliott Committee, including the abolition of the rank of Commandant outlined in this War Office letter to her of August 1943, heralded the end of Emma's war service.

Suddenly it was announced that the Admiralty was taking over Stranmillis Hospital and we were all to be transferred to Holywood. As Miss Irwin

---

[119] PRONI, D2109/20/5. Lady Edwina Mountbatten was Superintendent-in-Chief, St John Ambulance. On 5 June 1943, a letter from 'Commandant Emma S. Duffin to The Lady Louis Mountbatten, Lady Superintendent, St John Ambulance Brigade' expressed Emma's view that because 'the V.A.D.s … are now to hold the same rank as the A.T.S. do after six weeks, namely 'Nursing Orderlies' … in my opinion will inevitably lead to lack of discipline in the wards …. Needless to say I will loyally abide by the committee's decision and do my best to see my V.A.D.s accept its ruling. I make no secret of the fact that I anticipate resentment and dismay when they learn of it. I am, madam, Your obedient servant, E. S. Duffin.'

[120] D2109/20/5. The 'W.O. Memorandum for Miss E. S. Duffin 83/4714 (AMDI)' reads 'In a speech to the House of Commons on Tuesday 3 August 1943 the Secretary of State for War described the basis on which the recommendations of the Elliott Committee on the Voluntary Aid Detachments would be implemented …' and invited Emma to 'say whether you would be prepared to apply for appointment as Warrant Officer under this scheme so that your application might be considered with any other recommendations which may be made'.

was V.A.D. commandant there, there was nothing for me to do. We were billeted in quarters in the Barracks and fed in the Sisters' mess. Then it transpired that the C.O. in charge of the naval hospital at Stranmillis badly wanted V.A.D.s. He sent for me and asked me to get my V.A.D.s who had resigned to join the navy. I explained there was a clause in army regulations forbidding them to do so. He was furious and said he was going to London and would go to the Admiralty and War Office and insist on getting them, and he did, greatly to my delight. I found in peacetime he had been a member of St John.

I was longing to get my discharge but instead the Holywood hospital was transferred to Bangor and my remaining V.A.D.s with it, also any of the Holywood V.A.D.s who had stayed on and their Commandant, Miss Irwin, was demobbed. I look back at my time at Bangor with a feeling of disgust. I was told I was to be billeted with the sisters who had gone ahead. I made my way to the billets, a gloomy house in a side street. Not unnaturally, the sisters had already established themselves in the best rooms. I was shown the only one left, a tiny attic with an old iron bed and a chest of drawers. I confess my heart sank. At my quarters at Stranmillis I had had my own bedroom and sitting room. It is true as a V.A.D. in the first war I had had many uncomfortable billets but I was younger then. My sister Celia Randall, who lived in Holywood, said 'Why not get permission to live with us and go in on the bus?' I followed the suggestion and put it before Col. Lambkin, the C.O. He said he saw no object as long as I did not claim billeting or travel allowance. I agreed to this and felt rather cheered. I then proceeded to explore the V.A.D.s' billets. I found there was no room or office allotted to me. The V.A.D.s' quarters were in the main body of the hospital. A large room was divided into a kitchen and dining room. There was no sitting room and this 1/2 room was to serve me as my only room too. The V.A.D.s slept in small empty wards and a large Nissen hut. Their food was cooked in the hospital kitchen by one of the V.A.D. cooks at first but later they had to join the A.T.S. Undoubtedly they had been rather spoilt at Stranmillis and had had a civilian cook who had gone out of her way to make them good puddings and cakes and had done wonders with the rations. Their meals had been served properly in a dining room; now they had to carry their own knife, fork and spoon and sit on a wooden bench. It is true so did the A.T.S.s but the V.A.D.s were nurses and had been enlisted as such. They had been ready and were called up at the beginning of both wars and they got a poor return. They were discontented and unhappy and so

Inver Museum Collection of St John Ambulance Memorabilia

THE ST. JOHN & RED CROSS **HOSPITAL LIBRARY**

There are many people for whom the war has not yet ended . . . the lame heroes of Dunkirk, Tobruk, Alamein, Normandy, the Rhine, of Coventry, London and other war shattered towns. Do you remember them . . . *do you?*

The St. John & Red Cross is still working for them, and the Hospital Library Department needs your help—your books—to carry on. This Department must collect, repair where necessary, and distribute at least 100,000 books every month to ensure adequate service. In over 2,000 hospitals, libraries have been established, staffed with St. John & Red Cross Hospital Librarians.

It is a tremendous undertaking, but it must be maintained . . .

PLEASE SEND THIS BOOK TO

THE ST. JOHN & RED CROSS HOSPITAL LIBRARY OLD MUSEUM BUILDINGS 7, COLLEGE SQUARE NORTH BELFAST

Emma S. Duffin
V.A.D Commandant
Stranmillis Military Hospital
St. John Ambulance Belfast

was I. Some of the V.A.D. clerks were billeted in an empty villa the other side of Bangor and I rather enjoyed the walk across to inspect the quarters though I could do little when I got there. All the V.A.D.s' papers were taken from me to the Company office and I hung about aimlessly with nothing to do. I was thankful to get home in the evenings to the Randalls at Holywood.

The hospital was all being re-arranged and the V.A.D.s were constantly being moved from one part to another. At a moment's notice I had to transfer them all to vacant Nissen huts. I tried to fix up a sitting room but the hut was taken over just as I'd made it fairly comfortable. They had nowhere to go when off duty. Then they were moved to the top floor of Lord Clanmorris's house which had been taken over. I thought at last they'd got better quarters and with the help of two charwomen I got the place cleaned up but hardly had I done so than I was told they were to go to an hotel which had been taken over for the A.T.S. I made my way to the hotel where I found Lady Brookeborough who in the capacity of a Welfare Officer was inspecting it.[121] She agreed with me that the quarters allotted to the V.A.D.s were quite inadequate and said she would do what she could. Whether she accomplished anything I don't know for at last my papers came through. I was 'demobbed'.

I was thankful to shake the dust off my feet but sorry that my career with the army after two wars should end so unsatisfactorily. But the war was drawing to a close and it would only have been a question of a month or so before I would have been leaving anyway. The Colonel and Capt. Johnston both wrote me very nice letters thanking me for the service I had done. I said goodbye to my remaining V.A.D.s and went home.

---

[121] Lady Cynthia Mary Brooke (later Lady Brookeborough) (1897–1970) was the wife of Sir Basil Brooke who had become Prime Minister of Northern Ireland in May 1943.

BIBLIOGRAPHY

Jonathan Bardon, *A History of Ireland in 250 Episodes* (Dublin, 2008)

Jonathan Bardon, *A History of Ulster* (Belfast, 1992)

Thomas Bartlett and Keith Jeffery, *A Military History of Ireland* (Cambridge University Press, 1997)

Brian Barton, *Brookeborough. The Making of a Prime Minister* (Belfast, 1988)

    The Belfast Blitz. The city in the war years (Belfast, 2015)

    Northern Ireland in the Second World War (Belfast, 1995)

George Beal and Eamon Phoenix, eds., *Stran. Stranmillis College 1922–1998. An Illustrated History* (Belfast, 1998)

Paula Beaumont and Hilary Maginnis, eds., *Princess Gardens School. A Goodly Heritage* (Belfast, 1993)

John William Blake, *Northern Ireland in the Second World War* (Belfast, 1956)

Richard Broad and Suzie Fleming, eds., *Nella Last's war, The Second World War Diary of Housewife No. 49* (London, 2006)

H. Rex Cathcart. *The Most Contrary Region: The BBC in Northern Ireland 1924–1984.* (Belfast, 1984)

Catherine Charley, *Vision and Venture. A History of the Bryson Charitable Group 1906–2006. 100 years of Voluntary Service in Belfast and Northern Ireland* (Belfast, 2006)

James Doherty, *Post 381: The Memoirs of a Belfast Air Raid Warden* (Belfast, 1989)

Robert Harbinson, *Song of Erne* (London, 1960)

Deirdre Heenan and Derek Birrell, *Social Policy in Northern Ireland: Conflict and Change* (Bristol, 2011)

N. C. Fleming, *The Marquess of Londonderry. Aristocracy, Power and Politics in Britain and Ireland* (London, 2005)

Christopher McGimpsey, *A Camera Record. Bombs on Belfast. The Blitz 1941* (Belfast, 1984)

Gillian McLelland and Diana Hadden, *Pioneering Women. Riddel Hall and Queen's University Belfast* (Belfast, 2005)

William Maguire, *Belfast. A History* (Lancaster, 2009)

H. Montgomery Hyde, *The Londonderrys. A Family Portrait* (London, 1979)

Brian Moore, *The Emperor of Ice Cream* (London, 1967)

John A Oliver, *Working at Stormont* (Dublin, 1978)

Philip Ollerenshaw, *Northern Ireland in the Second World War. Politics, Economic Mobilisation and Society, 1939–45* (Manchester, 2013)

R. W. M. Strain, *Belfast and its Charitable Society. A Story of Urban Social Development* (Oxford University Press, 1961)

Peter Smyth, *Changing Times. Life in 1950s Northern Ireland* (Colourpoint Books, Newtownards, 2012)

INDEX

Trevor Parkhill was born in Coleraine
in 1950 and educated at Millburn
Primary School, Coleraine Academical
Institution and Queen's University
Belfast. Following a spell as archivist
in Dublin, with the Irish Manuscripts
Commission, he taught history in
Belfast Royal Academy before moving
in 1974 to the Public Record Office
of Northern Ireland. In 1995 he was
appointed Keeper of History, Ulster
Museum, retiring in 2012. He has
been Chair of the Board of Governors
of Hazelwood Integrated College,
north Belfast, since 1999 and was
recently (2015) appointed M.B.E for
services to education. He and his wife
Sheila are especially proud of their
grandchildren, Eimhir, Conor,
Ronan, Killian and Riain.